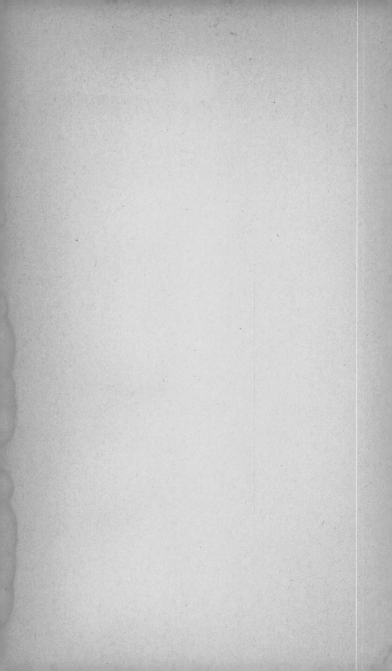

THE BEHAVIORAL
PERSUASION IN POLITICS

STUDIES IN
POLITICAL
SCIENCE

THE
BEHAVIORAL
PERSUASION
IN POLITICS

HEINZ EULAU
STANFORD UNIVERSITY

RANDOM HOUSE

New York

TO

Harold D. Lasswell, *Persuader*

PREFACE

New ways of saying and doing things have always tempted some and terrified others. The citizens of Athens once put to death a sage named Socrates, charging "corruption of the young," and "neglect of the gods when the city worships, and the practice of religious novelties." Both charges were, and remain, somewhat obscure. It seems that Socrates, among other crimes, had introduced a new, critical method into philosophical speculation. And politics was among the topics he considered.

In politics, methods of study and objectives of inquiry are particularly subject to controversy. The stakes are probably higher in politics than in any other field of human effort, and today that even includes religion. New approaches and objectives are likely to arouse passions. Indeed, so much so that some people believe disinterested political inquiry to be impossible. Of course, the innovator is no longer forced to drink hemlock, at least not in societies that take pride in free investigation. Instead he becomes involved in interminable debate with his critics.

Perhaps it is best, therefore, to state my case at the very outset by describing what this book is not.

This is not a tract in political polemics. There has been, as there should be, a great deal of dispute about what I shall call the behavioral persuasion in politics, but I mean to ignore it. More often than not, the debate has been about the possibility of having a value-free science of politics. The question is not unique to the study of politics, and though I think it is important, I have never found the polemics in its wake very profitable.

Nor is this book a programmatic statement, an agenda of things to do and how to do them. Although programming is an important element in the strategy of scientific research, the purely programmatic phase of the behavioral persuasion in politics has passed. For the interested reader I shall list some early programmatic statements in the bibliography to the Introduction.

Nor is this book a critical inventory of political behavior research. In a rapidly growing and changing area of investigation, inventories are urgently needed. But since there is a great division of labor in research in political behavior, the preparation of adequate inventories requires the collaboration of several specialists. Again, the interested reader will find listings of useful inventories in the bibliographies attached to the different chapters.

Finally, this is not a text about political behavior. The behavioral persuasion in the study of politics is quite young, and though there has been a great deal of behavioral research on politics in recent years, there is not yet enough. Various topics have been unevenly treated, and the findings are very tentative. I must confess to prejudice against texts in a field that is still so wide open. Texts often give the impression of knowledge where, in fact, it is lacking.

This book *is*, I hope, an essay, as defined by the dictionary: "a literary composition, analytical or interpretative, dealing with its subject from a more or less limited or personal standpoint." It does not pretend to be wise or erudite, nor to be systematic, comprehensive, or exhaustive. I have not reviewed the literature nor consulted my own voluminous files, though I occasionally reread my earlier comments on the subject. I wrote this book as a personal document, off the cuff, setting down what came to mind as it derived from my experiences in political life, in reading, in teaching, and in research.

Although there are no quotations or citations, I am deeply indebted to the many scholars who make this intellectual venture possible. The behavioral study of politics is a truly collaborative effort. The bibliographies which follow each chapter are meant to acknowledge this debt. If I do not identify the particular sources in the text, neither do I presume to originality. Much of what I write here has been said before. I am merely trying to say it in as simple and personal a way as I can.

However, the one source which I must acknowledge is Harold Lasswell, to whom I have dedicated this essay. His work has been a continuing source of stimulation and suggestion. But I am not a disciple. Indeed, one of the admirable things about Lasswell's teaching is that it makes discipleship impossible. Perhaps the greatest compliment I can pay him is to say that he has been, and still is, the gadfly of American political science, the one Young Turk who can be counted on to stay that way. His influence is pervasive.

This book reflects my didactic approach to political behavior. I say very little about teaching, a good deal about research. Yet the three middle chapters correspond in title to the three undergraduate courses I offered at Stanford University between 1958 and 1961. Of course, the material covered in a college course over a period of several months cannot be repeated in a chapter of only a few thousand words. For both individual study and class discussion these courses depended heavily on reports of empirical research. It has always seemed to me that the process by which knowledge about politics, or anything else, is created is as important from the teaching point of view as such knowledge itself. Students, by being allowed to read and study empirical research reports, may learn how very little is as yet *known* about political be-havior, how difficult it is to come by *reliable* political knowledge, and how tricky the problems and dilemmas of a science of politics really are.

This, in short, presents an orientation to the study of politics that, in some respects, has come to be a way of life.

Stanford, California   HEINZ EULAU

CONTENTS

THE BEHAVIORAL
PERSUASION IN POLITICS

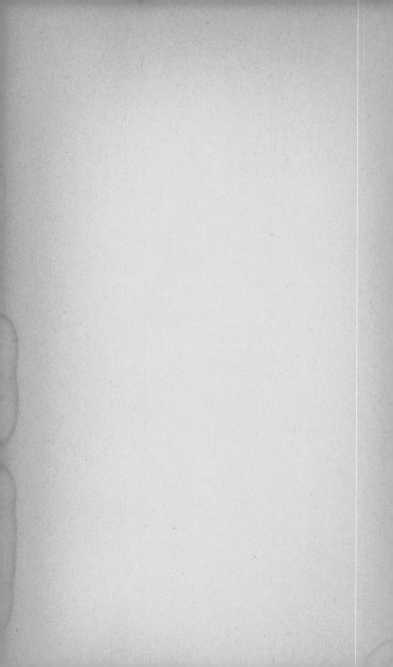

❀ ❀

THE ROOT IS MAN

The root is man. I don't think it is possible to say anything meaningful about the governance of man without talking about the political behavior of man—his acts, goals, drives, feelings, beliefs, commitments, and values. Man has built nations and empires, created customs and institutions, invented symbols and constitutions, made wars, revolutions, and peace. Politics is the study of why man finds it necessary or desirable to build government, of how he adapts government to his changing needs or demands, of how and why he decides on public policies. Politics is concerned with the conditions and consequences of human action.

A study of politics which leaves man out of its equations is a rather barren politics. Yet such is the propensity of man that he can consider his own creations without measuring them by himself. Political science has studied political ideas, values, customs, symbols, institutions, processes, and policies without reference to their creators for a long time, but the cost has been high. I do not want to belabor this point. I mention it only because the simple question I want to ask—Why do people behave politically as they do?

—seems to have explosive consequences for the study of politics.

Just what *is* political behavior? I have been asked the question many times, by students as well as by colleagues, in and out of political science. Is it a field of study, a method, or an approach? If it is a field, it must have content and boundaries. If it is a method, it must have rules. If it is an approach, it must have direction. I cannot say that it is one or the other. It is none of them alone, and it is not all of them together. This leaves the questioner confused, perhaps irritated, even hostile. It is not considered a virtue to tolerate ambiguity. I would certainly not argue that ambiguity is preferable to clarity, though it may be preferable to false or easy answers.

The difficulty begins with definitions. If taken seriously, definitions commit and constrain. They orient their user and reveal his orientation. They are embedded in his concepts and his theorizing, are a source of sense, but also of nonsense. So it is with "political behavior." For some years now, I have asked my students to define politics. Politics, they tell me, has something to do with government, power, policy, influence, decision making, conflict, or even "authoritative allocation of values." I cannot but marvel at such ingenuity. But when I ask just what people *do* when they *act* in ways to which these concepts presumably refer, there is a perplexing silence.

I wonder why this is so. Evidently, we are the victims of our own sophistication. However, this is not the case when I ask what people do when they practice religion. The students will tell me that a man is religious when he prays, attends mass, sings hymns, listens to sermons, immerses himself in baptismal water, senses the presence of divine guidance, abides by the Ten Commandments, or believes in immortality. And there is no trouble with economics: man produces, buys, sells, exchanges, invests, speculates, consumes, and so on. Not so with politics. When I suggest that what makes man's behavior political is that he rules and obeys, persuades and compromises, promises and bargains, coerces and represents, fights and fears, my students are baffled.

Certainly these verbs do not define politics. But they do refer to those of man's acts that are at the core of what we study when we talk about politics. And there are many more. If human behavior is the root of politics, they are more useful in studying political things than nouns like authority, power, conflict, allocation, or government. It seems to me that behavior comes first: ruling before government, obeying before authority, voting before decision, demanding before value, fearing before sanction, coercing before power, persuading before influence, fighting before conflict, believing before ideology.

But such is the enterprise, whether we call it politics, political study, or political science, that we must define first and then sense, rather than sense first and then define. As we define politics, so we behave politically, for our definitions of politics are themselves evidence of political behavior. They determine, at least in part, what we observe and how we explain it. It would be silly to deny that man in politics, being a defining animal, has various definitions of politics. I am merely pleading that in seeking, clarifying, or refining our definitions of politics, we turn to what men do as they behave politically and why they do it. Definitions unrelated to the behavior of man, in politics as in any other area of human activity, have no content.

The behavioral persuasion in politics is concerned with what man does politically and the meanings he attaches to his behavior. Politics asks about ancient traditions and grandiose designs, about complex systems and intricate processes, about fearful atrocities and superb achievements. But as an eminent physicist once remarked, it is a subject "more difficult than physics." The physical scientist seems to have one great advantage over the political scientist: whatever meanings he may give his objects of study, they do not talk back to him. Atoms, neutrons, or electrons do not care how they are defined; political actors do mind.

This is precisely why a political science that ignores man is necessarily a very incomplete science of politics.

However, the fact that men give meanings to their behavior need not be a handicap. On the contrary, what men say about themselves and others represents an infinitely rich source of information about behavior. And the meanings that people give to politics are appropriate data for scientific analysis because people behave in terms of these meanings. These meanings do not provide the scientific observer with the kind of definitions he needs in order to proceed with his investigation. He must develop his own. But, whatever definition of politics the political scientist adopts, it cannot be altogether arbitrary. It must itself be "meaningful" in terms of the meanings that men give to their political behavior. In the language of science, definitions must be operational. No matter how concrete or abstract conceptually, they must be relevant empirically. The meanings that political actors, consciously or unconsciously, attribute to their own behavior are of interest to the political scientist because they provide a partial explanation of the motives for that behavior.

Defining political behavior is a delicate problem, partly because people in politics define and interpret what they do differently, and partly because political scientists are by no means agreed on what they mean when they say that they are studying political behavior. One way to avoid the dilemma is to ignore it, offer a definition as succinctly as possible, and go on from there. The researcher must do this. He cannot get entangled in problems of definition if he hopes to come up with a piece of research. The only criterion is that his definition suit his research objectives, and this is probably all that can be reasonably expected. The problem of definition must ultimately be solved by empirical research.

A rigorous approach to definitions alone will not spur progress in the study of politics. In fact it might well stifle in infancy a new approach which requires not definitional rigor so much as new categories and concepts with which to explore new terrain. In returning to the behavior of man as the root of politics, the behavioral persuasion has opened up new possibilities in the study of politics. If this has created more problems than it has solved, including those of definition, it is more of a challenge than a defeat.

The return to the behavior of man as the root of politics is a new beginning. For in dealing with the conditions and consequences of man's political conduct, the behavioral persuasion represents an attempt, by modern modes of analysis, to fulfill the quest for political knowledge begun by the classical political theorists. The behavioral persuasion in politics, as I understand it, is a return to the bases of man's political experience in which the great theorists of the past found nurture and sustenance. What makes the so-called classic theories great are their sometimes explicit, sometimes implicit assumptions about human nature in politics. The theoretical constructions of the polity found in the classics are "peopled systems," model communities based on some notion of how men behave politically as they do and why, in addition to frequently being prescriptions for how men ought to behave in the polity and what the polity should look like. Of course, the psychology, sociology, and even anthropology involved in these images is, from the contemporary perspective, primitive, underdeveloped, and often mistaken. I certainly do not advise a reading of the classics for the purpose of learning about political behavior, not even of the empirical Machiavelli. But this is not the point. The point is that classical political theory, as the modern behavioral persuasion in politics, has at its base the conduct of man, even if, counter to the behavioral persuasion, it is predominantly prescriptive rather than descriptive.

It may seem startling that the behavioral persuasion is a continuation of the classical tradition of political inquiry. On the face of things, the discontinuities between the ancient and the modern approaches seem more significant than the continuities. Modern modes of thought, criteria of validation, and methods of investigation are so radically different that the link between classical political theory and the behavioral persuasion would seem to be rather tenuous. A good deal depends on what one means by continuity. If one means continued textual exegesis of the classics as if they were sacred writings, the behavioral persuasion does, in fact, make a radical break with political theory. But if by continuity one means, as I think one should, the application of modes of thought and techniques of inquiry appropriate to one's own time to the political problems of the time, then the behavioral persuasion is a direct and genuine descendant of the classical tradition. The classical theorists, from Plato to Mill and beyond, in building their models of the polity, sought to bring to political inquiry the best conceptual and technical tools at their disposal. The modern political scientists who adapt the new theories, methods, and techniques of behavioral science to political analysis are in the tradition of the classical political theorists.

Concern with the political behavior of man has posed the following questions: Does it encourage dealing in trivia while the "really important" problems of politics are neglected? Does it not lead to cultivating areas of research where access to data is easy, regardless of the "significance" of the political problem? What does political behavior research contribute to the solution of the great issues of politics? These questions are not so much unwarranted as they are misdirected. It is perfectly true that much behavioral research on politics is concerned with simple questions. But a simple question is not necessarily a simple matter. The line between asking simple but important questions and asking trivial ones is often very narrow. Moreover, there is much confusion as to just what "significance" means. If it is *only* defined in terms of the so-called great issues, then politics as science is likely to become the handmaiden of policy, for better or for worse (*see the Epilogue*). But whatever other relevance the great-issues criterion may have, it does not necessarily help to define significance from the point of view of political behavior research.

A question may be simple, then, without being trivial. From the standpoint of empirical research, it is trivial only if it does not yield answers that "significantly" add to knowledge. In fact, many answers given to questions, simple or complex, from the point of view of policy, do not add to knowledge. By knowledge I mean, of course, a set of verified statements about reality. If the statements hang together and do not contradict each other, we have knowledge. This is as true of politics as of any other area of human endeavor.

Now, the interesting thing about this chain of reasoning is that it is based on hindsight, although when we call a question trivial, we speak as if we had foresight. This is so because knowledge is transmitted. A trivial question is one we assume has been answered already, or, if it has not been answered, that it can be answered easily enough. A trivial question, it is implied, is one that every fool can answer. We simply predict, from hindsight, that a trivial question will not significantly contribute to new knowledge.

However this approach to knowledge does not lead anywhere. Knowledge is the process of knowing, always undergoing change. If this is so, we cannot call a question trivial, for we cannot *know* whether it is trivial or not until it has been asked and answered. Triviality is not a matter of the kind of *questions* we ask, but of the *answers* we get. Only after a question has been answered can we say that it has been trivial. Without an answer, one can call a question trivial only if one assumes that everything worthy of being known is known already. It is sometimes advantageous to assume that we don't know what we think we know. In other words, it may sometimes be advisable to ask old questions as if they were fresh.

It is the function of science to understand and interpret the world, not to change it. A science of politics which deserves its name must build from the bottom up by asking simple questions that can, in principle, be answered; it cannot be built from the top down by asking questions that, one has reason to suspect, cannot be answered at all, at least not by the methods of science. An empirical discipline is built by the slow, modest, and piecemeal cumulation of relevant theories and data. The great issues of politics, such as the conditions and consequences of freedom, justice, or authority, are admittedly significant topics, but they are topics compounded with a strong dose of metaphysical discourse. I don't think that they are beyond the reach of behavioral investigation, but before they can be tackled, the groundwork must be laid.

There is little glory to be had in the patient analysis of mass political behavior (and elite behavior is, indeed, much more glamorous as a topic of inquiry). But the hundreds of studies of electoral behavior, some good, some not, accumulated in the last sixty years, allow us to make some statements about democracy that are true with a reasonably high degree of probability, certainly higher than if these studies had not been made. This is all one can hope for in the present stage of political inquiry, an early stage in spite of the great thinkers who have influenced our notions of significance. But we cannot decide whether an Aristotle's concerns should be our concerns by appealing to Aristotle. We can decide this only by questioning our own experiences in the world of politics in which we live. If our experiences lead us back to the great issues, all to the good; if they do not, little is lost.

In returning to man as the root of politics, the behavioral persuasion reveals itself as a "radical" orientation in the study of politics. But its practitioners are neither wide-eyed prophets nor blind apostles. They are self-consciously sensitive to the difficulties involved in the behavioral study of politics. The way ahead is never clear or straight. One may not always know the destination, and even if in sight, one may never reach it. But it makes an exciting journey, if not always a rewarding one.

What the behavioral persuasion challenges in the traditional study of politics, if it challenges anything, is the comfortable assumption that theory is the same thing as knowledge. But theory is only a tool. If it is a tool, like all tools it tends periodically to wear out and need replacement. The behavioral persuasion in politics is both theoretical and empirical in direction. Its radicalism stems from the conviction that a proposition may be worn out when, on being tested, it can be disproved.

BIBLIOGRAPHY

PROGRAMMATIC STATEMENTS OF THE BEHAVIORAL PERSUASION

Catlin, George E. G., *Science and Method of Politics*. (New York: Knopf, 1927.)

Lasswell, Harold D., *The Analysis of Political Behavior: An Empirical Approach*. (New York: Oxford, 1948.)

Merriam, Charles E., *New Aspects of Politics*. (Chicago: University of Chicago Press, 1925.)

Rice, Stuart A., *Quantitative Methods in Politics*. (New York: Knopf, 1928.)

COLLECTIONS OF POLITICAL BEHAVIOR RESEARCH

Eulau, Heinz, Eldersveld, Samuel J., and Janowitz, Morris (eds.), *Political Behavior: A Reader in Theory and Research*. (New York: Free Press, 1956.)

Fiszman, Joseph R. (ed.), *The American Political Arena*. (Boston: Little, Brown, 1962.)

Ulmer, S. Sidney (ed.), *Introductory Readings in Political Behavior*. (Chicago: Rand McNally, 1961.)

Wahlke, John C., and Eulau, Heinz, (eds.), *Legislative Behavior: A Reader in Theory and Research*. (New York: Free Press, 1959.)

INVENTORIES OF GENERAL POLITICAL BEHAVIOR RESEARCH

Butler, David, *The Study of Political Behavior*. (London: Hutchinson, 1958.)

Ranney, Austin (ed.), *Essays on the Behavioral Study of Politics*. (Urbana: University of Illinois Press, 1962.)

Research Frontiers in Politics and Government, Brookings
    Lectures, 1955. (Washington, D.C.: Brookings Institution,
    1955.)
Waldo, Dwight, *Political Science in the United States: A
    Trend Report*. (Paris: UNESCO, 1956.)

CRITICAL COMMENTARIES ON THE BEHAVIORAL PERSUASION

Crick, Bernard, *The American Science of Politics*. (Berkeley:
    University of California Press, 1959.)
Storing, Herbert J. (ed.), *Essays on the Scientific Study of
    Politics*. (New York: Holt, Rinehart and Winston, 1962.)

CHAPTER ONE

✿ ✿

BEHAVIORAL

APPROACHES

The behavioral persuasion in politics has more than one approach, and there are many voices that speak in its name. But they all have in common a commitment to the study of man as the root of things political, or, to put it more technically, to the individual person as the empirical unit of analysis. Therefore I think it is legitimate to speak of "the behavioral persuasion in politics." However these voices do not necessarily speak in harmony. Behavioral researchers on politics differ among themselves in many respects: in their conception of the nature of knowledge and its relation to reality; in their formulation of the theoretical propositions guiding their investigations; in the choice of strategies and tactics of research; in their selection of problems and research sites and, finally, in their appraisal of their own role in relation to the world of politics they are studying. It seems preferable, therefore, to speak of behavioral approaches when it comes to technical matters.

I think that most behavioral researchers agree on at least four major aspects of the behavioral enterprise in politics, aspects that define the stance and style of those who subscribe to the behavioral persuasion. Each aspect involves a set of problems on which behavioral practitioners may differ, but which bind them precisely because they agree that the problems require solutions. First there is the problem of the most adequate theoretical (as against empirical) units of analysis. The second problem is the level of analysis on which political behavior research may be most fruitfully conducted. Third, there is the question of the proper relationship between theory and research. Finally, there is the problem of what methodological requirements should be met.

UNITS OF ANALYSIS

The political behavior of the individual person is the central and crucial empirical datum of the behavioral approaches to politics. This does not mean that research is restricted to the individual person as the theoretical focus of investigation. Indeed, most behavioral researchers are not concerned with the individual political actor as such. A small group, an organization, a community, an elite, a mass movement, or a nation may be the focus of behavioral inquiry and events, structures, functions, processes, or relations may serve as categories of behavioral analysis.

This does not imply that behavioral investigations dealing with units other than the individual actor "reduce" them to the level of the person. We mean different things when we say that an individual behaves in certain ways and that a nation behaves in certain ways. To speak of a nation's behavior in the conduct of its foreign relations is, quite clearly, to engage in metaphorical license, just as we do when we speak of the behavior of stars, storms, or stocks. The use of metaphors for the purpose of analogical thinking is feasible and even necessary, but it can be dangerous because it may make for a good deal of distortion. It is only too easy to speak of a group's or nation's behavior *as if* it were identical with that of the individual person. Consequently, inferences drawn from such practice are likely to be false.

The political behaviorist concentrates on the behavior of individuals whose interactions and transactions make up collective behavior, even if he is concerned with describing and explaining the actions of groups, organizations, or other large collectivities. Groups, organizations, or nations have no independent status apart from the conduct of the individuals who are related by behaving towards each other in certain ways. This does not mean that groups, organizations, or other formations are not "real" and meaningful units with structural properties and functions of their own. They certainly are. In fact, the great bulk of problems interesting the political scientist concerns the actions of such groups. But, from the behavioral perspective, these collectivities exist and behave the way they do only insofar as the people composing them act in certain ways.

In choosing the individual as his empirical unit of analysis, the political behaviorist does not deny the reality of institutions. He merely asserts that institutions do not and cannot exist physically apart from the persons who inhabit them. The political behaviorist is likely to stress this point because institutional and behavioral analyses have, at times, been treated as if they were opposed to each other. They are not. Political institutions are never more or less different from the patterns of behavior of the people who create them or the regularities of their actions. If this be so, institutions can and must be analyzed in terms of the behavior of their molecular units, the individuals whose relations to each other and behavior towards each other are more or less rigidly structured. We speak of "the opinion of a court," "the decision of a bureau," or "the action of a legislature" only because speaking in "institutional language" brings the great complexity of political life into a manageable perspective. Behind the opinions, decisions, or actions of institutions are human beings who decide, who have opinions, and who act.

When we say that the legislature makes the law of the land we really mean that most people affected by legislative action will be guided in their own conduct by what a majority of the legislators have agreed they must do or not do. The legislators themselves have acted as they did because they entertained reasonably stable expectations that most people whose behavior they are called on to guide will accept their decisions and, through conforming to them, confirm what, in institutional language, we call "the authority of the legislature." It is precisely because the behavioral patterns involved in this set of interpersonal relations are relatively uniform, regular, and stable that we can speak of the legislature as an institution.

Political institutions are behavior systems or systems of action. Just as they cannot exist apart from the persons whose behavior brings them into existence, so political behavior cannot exist apart from the network of interpersonal relations that we call political institutions. Presumably, political behavior has much in common with other types of social behavior, but the adjective "political" warns us that the behavior in question represents a special case. The difference is in the institutional setting of the behavior.

An attempt is sometimes made to define what seems to be political in behavior by identifying some special characteristic assumed to be inherent in behavior. For instance, interpersonal behavior constituting relations of "power" or "conflict" have been singled out as the characteristic features of *political* behavior. But power or conflict relations, though admittedly frequent in politics, are not exclusively political aspects of interpersonal actions. We can speak meaningfully of "economic power" or "racial conflict" without attributing peculiarly political characteristics to them. Otherwise almost all behavior could be called political and the term would lose whatever discriminatory meaning it may have. This does not mean that power or conflict cannot serve as useful organizing concepts. As such they may enable us to examine institutional settings for whatever generic features accompany the patterns of interpersonal relations and behavior to which they presumably refer. But I doubt that they are useful in specifying the context of political behavior.

Political seems to be a residual rather than a generic term. This makes it futile to search for characteristic features of political behavior apart from an institutional or situational environment that shapes and patterns certain types of interpersonal relations. Political behavior is invariably "electoral behavior," "administrative behavior," "judicial behavior," and so on. Or it is behavior relevant to the making of public policies, training the young in the norms of a group or society, recruiting people into political institutions, and so on. This implies that behavior in one context or institutional setting differs from behavior in others, and that the context or setting is the critical factor in political behavior.

There may be great similarities in the behavior of legislators, bureaucrats, judges, party leaders, and statesmen, or of agitators and revolutionaries, or of voters and nonvoters. But our concern is with those characteristics of behavior that we expect to occur because the behavior is relevant to the institutional political order of which it is a part. For this reason, political behavior is not a separate field of investigation. It would be meaningless to treat political behavior apart from situational conditions in the political order. Political scientists of the behavioral persuasion, whatever their approach, are not doing this. Rather, they select those behavioral patterns in the conduct of individual actors that pertain to particular political institutions or situations. Institutions differ in the structure of relations between individuals and the functions they perform in the political order. Inter-institutional analysis of political behavior can reveal, therefore, significant similarities or differences in political relations, between groups as much as between individuals. This type of analysis does not take politics out of behavior. On the contrary, it makes possible the behavioral analysis of institutions.

The relationship between institution and behavior is necessarily complementary. Institutional arrangements, norms, or functions express behavioral patterns that have been stabilized through the passage of time. In turn, current behavior is necessarily circumscribed and directed by the past patterns we call institutions. Institutions differ a great deal, of course, in the extent to which past behavior has been regularized and stabilized in terms of structures, functions, norms, or goals. As a result, different degrees of stability have a profound effect on what is presently mandatory, permissible, or prohibited behavior. In other words, institutional parameters of behavior are more or less rigid or flexible. A great deal can be discovered about these parameters by formal, institutional analysis. Whether and how much actual behavior conforms to or deviates from institutional prescriptions, regardless of whether they refer to structure, functions, norms, or goals, is of immediate interest to the behavioral researcher. He may discover politically significant discrepancies between what is thought to be relevant behavior and what the behavior actually is.

If the student of political behavior ignores the institutional sphere of politics, he imposes a severe handicap on his research. He sometimes does so because institutional parameters are so taken for granted that their consequences for current political behavior seem minimal. Whether they are or not is, of course, a matter of critical inquiry. In his haste to account for political behavior in social, cultural, or personal terms, the behavioral researcher may readily deceive himself by neglecting institutional analysis. A great deal of political behavior can be accounted for most economically by viewing it as a result of institutional prescriptions. To take a very simple and obvious case, electoral behavior is certainly influenced by the institutionalized characteristics of the party system or the representational system. Decision-making behavior in a legislative body differs from decision-making behavior in a bureaucratic setting. Behavior involving authority relationships is likely to be different in differently structured formal institutions: let us say, in a police department or a social welfare agency. No political behaviorist would be so foolish as to ignore the institutional environment in which behavior occurs, even though his main focus of attention is the individual actor rather than the institution.

LEVELS OF ANALYSIS

Despite the cliché, man is *not* a political animal by nature. If he is, he is only partly so. Of course, both the extent and the intensity of man's political participation vary a good deal in different persons, groups, and cultures. These variations may themselves be politically conditioned. Political institutions of different kinds set various requirements and limits on political behavior. In totalitarian systems, man's perspective of himself and his environment—his identifications, demands, and expectations—is more highly politicized than in more libertarian systems. Most facets of life are determined by the polity. But even in a totalitarian system there is likely to be some variance. Political parameters of an institutional sort cannot alone describe or explain variability in political behavior.

Because this is so, the behavioral persuasion in politics is not readily contained by the conventional, academic subject-matter boundaries. Its interdisciplinary orientation stems, at least initially, from the very simple assumption that man's political behavior is only one aspect of his total behavior, and by no means a very important aspect. If this is so, differences in political behavior must be sought in the whole human being. But no one discipline pretends to know man as a whole. This does not mean that we can know about political behavior only if we know about all aspects of human behavior. We can reasonably assume that political behavior is more closely related to some aspects of behavior than to others. Just what aspects of political and other behavior are to be related in a particular investigation depend on the problem at hand and the theoretical scheme for solving it. Being interdisciplinary means selecting from what is known about man those of his behavioral characteristics investigated by different behavioral sciences that seem to be especially relevant to the solution of political problems.

If one were to rank the reasons for the interdisciplinary orientation of the behavioral persuasion in politics, the borderline character of political behavior problems would have to be given high priority. The kind of problems that the political behaviorist formulates cannot be solved without recourse to the concepts and theories of the several behavioral sciences. Problems have a way of spilling over disciplinary boundaries. Attempts to solve them in terms of a single discipline's concerns are likely to be partial and unsatisfactory. For instance, elections cannot be studied fruitfully on the assumption that the voter is a rationally calculating, self-interested political man. But one need not assume the opposite and deny the rational interests of the voter as a family man, a wage earner or a church member. The question of how and why the voter decides as he does cannot be answered by abstracting his behavior in the voting booth from his total experience. His loyalties to family or class, his identifications with group or party, his career demands and expectations, his cultural milieu, and even his personality may have to be taken into account. The interdisciplinary orientation prevents neglect of the wider context in which political behavior takes place. It calls attention to the possible effects of social, cultural, and personal factors that, on the face of things, are not political as such.

This formulation may give the impression that what is political in behavior can somehow be separated out of what is social, cultural, and personal. Actually, what we call social, cultural, and personal pervades all behavior, including political behavior. Only for the purpose of inquiry do we think of what is social but not political, cultural but not political, or personal but not political as analytically distinct. It is more appropriate, therefore, to speak of levels of analysis—the social, cultural and personal levels—on which political behavior may be examined. A configurative analysis of political behavior cannot ignore any one of these levels, though a problem may be more effectively treated on one level than on another (see Chapters Two, Three, and Four).

The study of political behavior is concerned with the acts, attitudes, preferences, and expectations of man in political contexts. But there is little reason to assume that his behavior in politics is basically different from his behavior in other contexts. People who do not participate in the social life of their community or in voluntary associations are also likely to be politically apathetic. The problem of the union leader seeking a maximum of concessions at the bargaining table does not seem to differ significantly from the problem of the legislator seeking a maximum of advantages for his district. Both must satisfy their respective voters to keep their jobs. Although participation in private groups and bargaining with management are not political, there may be behavioral similarities from one institutional context to another that are politically relevant.

Similarities in behavior sensitize the observer to critical differences, once institutional contexts are varied. For instance, superficially viewed, the behavior of a bureaucrat in a public agency appears to be very similar to the behavior of his opposite number in a private organization. Much bureaucratic behavior can be explained in terms of generic characteristics that stem from structural similarities of different institutional settings. But there are differences of a personal or social nature that cannot be ignored. A bureaucrat working for a public agency may be quite differently motivated and have different career expectations than the bureaucrat working for a private firm, with determinable consequences for the organizaton of which each is a member. Or the fact that the public bureaucrat's actions are more likely to be scrutinized by legislators than the private bureaucrat's actions by stockholders may have behavioral consequences that only interdisciplinary inquiry, with a focus on different institutions, can harness.

An interdisciplinary orientation has value quite apart from its usefulness in a particular research situation. It points to the level of analysis on which research may be conducted most fruitfully. It saves the researcher from formulating particularistic hypotheses where generic ones may be more appropriate. It suggests to him the feasibility of controlling different institutional contexts in order to identify similar behavioral patterns, or of controlling behavioral patterns in order to examine their effects in different contexts.

Even if political problems and patterns of political behavior were totally different from problems and behavioral patterns in other contexts, theoretical formulations concerning human behavior are unlikely to coexist in splendid isolation. Theory found useful in one context will sooner or later fertilize investigations in other contexts. A theory's viability is best judged by its range of interdisciplinary applicability. If it contributes to the explanation of behavior in many different settings, political as well as non-political, the knowledge gained will be the more significant. A theory that explains more rather than less variance is preferable. For this reason, the behavioral researcher in politics is forever on the lookout for theoretical models developed in the other social sciences. If they apply to his own problems, he can be all the more certain that his work deals with a significant problem. And just as theory transcends conventional disciplinary boundaries, so does method (see Chapter Five.)

How far one should go along interdisciplinary routes depends largely on the particular research problem. Many problems in politics can be dealt with without recourse to theoretical propositions or empirical findings of other disciplines. A politician's attitudes towards constituents are likely to vary with the degree of competition in the district where he stands for election. The more competitive his district, the more likely it is that he will be accessible to conflicting interest groups, that he will seek to mediate political conflicts in terms of his appraisal of the relative strength of competing groups, and that he will try to explain his conduct in a way that will antagonize as few groups as possible. It would be most uneconomical and, in fact, expendable, to seek an explanation of such behavior on the level of the politician's personality. It would contribute little, if anything, to the problem of why politicians from competitive areas behave differently from politicians in non-competitive areas.

On the other hand, one might pose this problem: are men who seek public office in a competitive political environment different in their personalities from those who seek office in a non-competitive arena? In other words, does competition attract a different manner of man than non-competition? Just what is it that makes some men cherish and others avoid political battle? Answers to these questions would require the investigation of political attitudes in terms of personality.

The behavioral persuasion in politics has been especially criticized in this connection and charged with "reductionism": i.e., that an interdisciplinary orientation inevitably reduces the political to the social, cultural, or personal; that the political is taken out of political behavior. I do not believe that it is reduction, but rather an expansion of political relevance that marks the behavioral approaches. Just what *is* political in behavior cannot be determined by criteria of immanence. An immanent or essentialist definition of politics is a convenient and certainly an arbitrary way of limiting one's scope of inquiry. This is the traditional way of proceeding with an investigation. But it is just because the traditional method has been found wanting that it is no longer feasible to draw the boundaries of a research project in politics too rigidly. If it can be shown that explanation of things political is possible, if not necessary, on different levels of analysis, including that of personality, the product of inquiry is not the result of reduction but rather of expansion of the political arena.

The proposition that politics is not defined by immanent characteristics but by its problems inevitably channels disciplinary into interdisciplinary discourse. Once one approaches problems analytically rather than concretely, whether as a behaviorist or institutionalist, the interdisciplinary orientation makes for generic rather than special explanations. A generic explanation is undoubtedly preferable to a special one. Indeed, the generic perspective permits us to locate any special perspective, to see it, as the term suggests, as a special case. For instance, politics considered as a special kind of decision-making behavior is probably more fruitful than politics thought of as typically and uniquely power-centered behavior. Decision-making takes place in many areas of social action, the purchase of goods, the choice of an occupation, the judging of a beauty contest. These are all special cases, as is political decision-making. The political scientist is a step ahead of himself if, in dealing with political decision-making, he has a generic point of reference. Without it, he is likely to be provincial and limited in perspective.

THEORY AND RESEARCH

No piece of political behavior research is content to describe the universe of politics, no matter how realistic or reliable the description. The goal is the explanation of why people behave politically as they do, and why, as a result, political processes and systems function as they do. There are many methods of explanation. Whatever they are, they require theorizing activity. (I speak of "theorizing activity" rather than "theory" because it frees me from having to say what theory *is*. Any attempt to do so in an essay of this sort would be foolish. My interest is in what, generally, practitioners of the behavioral persuasion in politics *do* when they theorize, not in defining theory.)

What behavioral researchers do when they theorize—by which I mean, very tentatively, when they seek explanations of why people behave politically as they do—differs a good deal from one to the other. At one pole, some would probably say that they are not theorizing at all, but only describing what they see. They deceive themselves, for what they see depends on how they see it, and how they see it depends on images in their minds. These images may be very diffuse and hardly deserve being called theories. But they orient the observer, innocent as he may be of what he is doing and though he may be protesting his theoretical innocence. His work will not get him very far because, paradoxically, his very attempt at *only* describing what he sees is suspect. Did he really see all that could have been seen? What did he leave out? How did he order what he saw? Did this really follow that? On the whole, the overwhelming number of modern behavioral practitioners no longer plead theoretical innocence. More often than not, they seek to make explicit the assumptions and ways of thought that guide their work. This is what I have called theorizing activity, though it does not necessarily entail theory.

At the other pole are the builders of logically consistent, deductive models of political systems, perhaps theories in the sense that "formal truth" is the distinctive content of the theorizing activity in which model builders are engaged. There are not many practitioners of the behavioral persuasion in politics who believe that this is the right time for constructing logically closed, deductive pictures of the political process. I have a great deal of admiration for these efforts, but I must confess to some doubt, not because I question the practicality of formal models or their suggestiveness in research, but because I suspect they are not as theoretically pure as their creators insist. At least I cannot avoid the impression that behind the most formal models there lurk quite explicit images of empirical reality. In other words, just as pure empiricism has theoretical components, so pure theory has empirical components.

In my opinion, this is not a drawback. Out of this duality stems the conviction that, in the present stage of development, theory and research are necessarily interdependent, that theoretical questions must be stated in operational terms for the purpose of fruitful empirical research, and that, in turn, empirical findings should be brought to bear on the theoretical formulation of political problems. This does not deny the possibility of a high road to theorizing about political behavior and a low road. But I am not sure, if there are two roads, which is high and which is low, and I have a hunch that there are many roads in between that are more immediately viable. This is why it seems most feasible to attack the problems of political behavior research on as broad a theoretical front as possible. Whatever the weight given to one or another, it seems quite clear that if the condition of mutual interdependence between theory and research is to be achieved, some theorizing activity must precede empirical work if the latter is to be theoretically relevant, just as empirical considerations must enter theoretical efforts if hypotheses are to be tested by research.

Admittedly, theorizing must be sufficiently independent of operations to give it room in which to breathe. But it cannot be altogether separate from empirical research. One might argue, as some have, that the condition of interdependence is met, and that a theory's operational utility can be appraised, if it can be tested *in principle* by reference to empirical data. This may be a necessary condition, but is not a sufficient one. I cannot see how one can *know* in principle whether theoretical propositions are testable. For theory is not the same thing as knowledge. Whatever the plausibility or validity of theoretical speculations, they are not truths, full, partial, or probable. Theory is not knowledge but a tool on the road to knowledge, just as facts are not knowledge but only the raw materials to be molded, through theorizing activity, into statements acceptable as probably true, or at least not false, because they have been tested in the process of empirical research. It is the theoretician's responsibility not only to assert that his propositions can be tested, but to suggest *how* they can be tested. But not even this makes his propositions empirical, though it may make them empirically relevant.

It is this kind of thinking which produces the characteristic commitment of the behavioral persuasion to theorizing and research as mutually interrelated activities. But if theorizing and research cannot do without each other, they necessarily limit each other. As a result, the behavioral persuasion is characterized by a healthy respect for those problems that research bound by theory and theorizing bound by research entail. On the whole, political behavior research has been limited to relatively modest theoretical propositions. Theorizing activity has been tempered by recognition of obstacles in the collection of data and technical limitiations in the treatment of data. Above all, this theorizing of the "middle range," unlike theoretically innocent empiricism or empirically blind model building, has been concerned with viable problems, problems that are operationally manageable and likely to yield returns of a cumulative sort.

The theoretical quest of behavioral research on politics is complicated by having to satisfy two masters. On the one hand, political behavior is only a special case of human behavior. If this is so, any theorizing about political behavior must take account of behavioral theory as it develops in all the social sciences, and the findings of political behavior research cannot contradict findings about other aspects of human behavior. From this perspective, there is really no place for an independent general theory of politics. On the other hand, political behavior research is conducted within the large scale institutions and processes of politics. Insofar as there is a special theory of politics on this level of analysis, it must at least be relevant, if not applicable, on the level of the individual. Not much progress has been made as yet along these lines.

Commitment to the interdependence of theory and research and to solving the problem of the relationship between special political and general behavioral theory has some interesting consequences for the development of political theory. The behavioral persuasion, in attending to both theory and empirical research, may bring the definitional game that has been played so long in the study of politics to some conclusion. However one defines politics, as the process of allocating values authoritatively, as a competitive struggle for power, as collective decision making for the community, and so on, each definition includes more or less well articulated premises, postulates, or assumptions about politics. One function of behavioral theorizing, certainly, is to lay bare these premises. Another is to clarify the empirical referents of concepts, definitions, and propositions. The notion that politics is an allocative process, for instance, assumes that resources are scarce and may be used in alternate ways. It further assumes that the goals are multiple and that, therefore, choices must be made among them. This definition also implies that political actors will disagree over what ends are preferable, as well as over how resources are to be allocated in order to achieve agreed on ends.

It is evident that we are not dealing here simply with a primitive definition of politics, but with a model of the political process borrowed from economics. On closer inspection, it also appears that the model makes assumptions about human rationality and about the behavior of rational human beings. And rational behavior is assumed to maximize preferred returns on the investment of resources. It is not accidental, therefore, that the definition of politics as "authoritative allocation of values" is readily translated into an even more formal model of the political process as a chain of inputs and outputs.

In subjecting the model to empirical testing, behavioral research alone can give the theorist some feeling as to what concept or definition is operationally useful and what is not. The specification of the empirical data needed to test a model may reveal which of rival definitions are serviceable and which are expendable. It may show which definitions are empirically, and possibly theoretically, necessary for each other. For instance, I have found in some of my own work on legislative behavior and institutions that a definition of politics as allocation is insufficient unless it is implemented by some definition of politics as conflictual behavior.

Moving simultaneously along both theoretical and empirical paths quickly sensitizes the investigator to what definitions, concepts, or even theories are expendable. For instance, it seems that power, long accepted as the central organizing concept of politics, is rapidly losing ground from the point of view of its operational, if not analytical, utility. Paradoxically, it is losing ground not because it is abused, as it has been by some theoreticians in the past, but because it is used. For as it is used in empirical research, it proves increasingly useless. In recent years, there has been much research interest in community power structures and in power relations in legislative bodies. We now have a large body of research findings as to how, presumably, decisions are made in villages, cities, and metropolitan areas, as well as in legislatures. The more research there is, the more elusive the concept of power shows itself to be.

I am not thinking here of the many methodological and technical difficulties that have been found to stand in the way of operationally defining, identifying, discovering and measuring "power." What I find interesting is that those engaged in power research are increasingly forced to rethink the concept as they face empirical situations that defy its traditional verbal uses. We now find distinctions made between the weight, scope, and domain of power, or between "monolithic" and "polylithic" power. Whether these distinctions and elaborations will save the concept as a theoretically useful one I cannot say. As used to be the case with the concept of "sovereignty" (unlimited and limited, undivided and divided, shared and what not), power is still a concept we cannot do much with apparently, but which we do not dare to do without.

Theorizing depends on the problem to be solved. Some

problems are more complex than others, and more may be known about simpler ones. Political behavior involved in the conduct of foreign policies in the international arena is probably more complex than behavior in the domestic legislative process, and the latter is likely to be more complex than a person's behavior in the voting booth. How complexity is handled depends, in turn, on the model used in the analysis of empirical data. Although a simple model is preferable to a complicated one, it is also likely to be empirically more exclusive. On the other hand, an elaborate model or conceptual scheme may make the problem technically unmanageable. Just as the analysis of only two variables that are theoretically linked in rather simple propositions may not explain very much, a comprehensive scheme of a potentially all-inclusive range may defy the practicalities of research. The most feasible alternative is to deal with modest propositions that require simultaneous manipulation of only a few variables, but to do so in a larger conceptual system that, though it cannot be tested directly, serves the very useful purpose of guiding an investigation and giving it theoretical significance.

Considerations of this kind have some further consequences for the development of behavioral theory in connection with problems of varying degrees of complexity. The more complex the empirical problem with which the research is dealing, the more difficult access to relevant behavioral data is likely to be, and the more need there will be for theoretical exploration on high levels of generality. On the other hand, the less complex the empirical problem, the easier the collection of relevant data and the less incentive to theorize. Therefore, theoretical formulations will be very specific and of relatively low generality. This makes plausible the theoretical unevenness of behavioral research in different, substantive areas of political science. In recent years, the behavioral persuasion has generated a considerable body of theoretical work of high generality in the study of international politics, but it has so far produced little *hard* empirical research. On the other hand, empirical studies of electoral behavior are abundant, but this research has been limited to testing very modest propositions of low theoretical generality, and no comprehensive theory of the electoral process has as yet been formulated.

This produces an interesting paradox. It would seem much more reasonable to apply and test theoretical models of high generality in relatively simple research areas about which a good deal is already known and where access to data is relatively easy. For instance, many of the models of international politics could be tested with data drawn from the political life of metropolitan areas. It would also seem more reasonable to cope with behavior in a complex setting by way of more modest theoretical propositions. Some of the work now being done on the national level in underdeveloped areas seems to be of this order. I believe this exchange of complex and simple theoretical formulations between different empirical research fields will be the next major phase in political behavior research, if it has not already begun. Students of international political behavior and large-scale institutional behavior will find it increasingly profitable to deal with propositions that have been found serviceable in studies of voting or problem-solving behavior in small groups. Students of relatively small institutions (such as legislative bodies or courts) and local communities will draw increasingly on the more comprehensive formulations of communication theory, system theory, and other configurative models.

BEHAVIORAL METHODS

The revolution in the behavioral sciences has been predominantly a technological revolution. Compared with developments in the natural sciences, the gimmicks and gadgets of behavioral science remain rather crude. But compared with the tools available to the classical writers, modern behavioral technology represents an enormous advance. It would seem foolish not to apply this new behavioral technology to the problems of politics. Yet, for reasons difficult to pin down, the application of behavioral methods to politics has been halting and circumspect. In some quarters, there has been fierce resistance to increasing our knowledge about politics through behavioral analysis. Why such resistance occurs is a matter of interest to the sociologist of knowledge, and how it might be overcome is a task for the psychoanalyst. The result is that the behavioral persuasion in politics is regarded, by its opponents as well as by its practitioners, as a revolt against the classical tradition in political science. As I suggested earlier, this is a mistake. If the behavioral persuasion revolted against anything, it was against the failure of academic political science to use the modern technology in the study of politics as, I believe, the classical writers would have used it had it been available to them.

Resistance to the application of behavioral methods must be distinguished from some very real difficulties of a methodological sort that the behavioral persuasion faces and with which I deal in the last chapter. I would now like to ask if there are not some "natural limits" to the behavioral analysis of politics, limits that no technological revolution can eradicate. I believe this question can be asked only if one assumes, *a priori,* that there *must* be aspects of political behavior intrinsically immune to scientific analysis. But if one assumes the opposite, that political behavior, like all behavior, can be observed by the methods of behavioral science, the limits appear to be technological ones. Scientific technology knows its present limits; it cannot predict its future limits. As technology advances, the range of phenomena amenable to scientific analysis also expands. Therefore, it is really impossible to say that the data of politics are such that they cannot be harnessed by *any* scientific methods and techniques. The presently available technology has made possible the production and processing of political data, or data relevant to political behavior, that was, until recently, unavailable to political science.

This is not the place to review the areas of political behavior research investigated by the techniques of modern behavioral science nor to present an inventory of research methods. The interested reader may wish to consult the bibliography. But I do want to emphasize the discovery and amplification of knowledge about politics which the invention of new methods and techniques makes possible.

The development of the probability sample survey as a reliable instrument of data collection is perhaps most noteworthy. It has made public opinion and electoral research a prolific source of political data. Indeed, for a time, the study of political behavior was equated with and restricted to the study of public opinion and voting But more recently, the extension of systematic surveys to the study of specialized elites and institutionalized groups like legislative bodies or bureaucratic organizations has greatly augmented the store of political data and deepened political analysis. The use of panels of informants, repetitively interviewed in successive waves, has added a longitudinal dimension to behavioral inquiry of politics. Political change can now be observed at the level of the individual actor.

Perhaps equally significant is the invention of metric techniques such as scalogram and factor analysis, and their application not only in survey materials, but also in the treatment of legislative roll-call votes or judicial decisions. Although the individual actor's behavior is known in political action of this kind, it cannot be analyzed meaningfully from the perspective of politics as a collective enterprise unless it can be ordered to reveal underlying regularities and uniformities. Scale analysis, for instance, makes possible the ordering of discrete acts like roll-calls along a single dimension and the classification of actors in terms of their scale positions. It provides for criteria of reliability in such ordering and constitutes an instrument of considerable analytic and predictive power. Similarly, factor analysis of judicial opinions, for instance, makes possible the discovery of the principal components of any set of interrelated decisions. The discovery of regularities and uniformities in judicial behavior made possible by factor analysis gives depth to the study of courts as political institutions.

The analysis of political group behavior has been facilitated by observational techniques recording both form and content of action-in-interaction at the level of the individual. Though few ongoing ("natural") political groups have as yet been subjected to one or another observational technique, it promises rich returns once small groups like legislative committees, administrative bodies, or party councils allow themselves to be systematically studied. The application of sociometric techniques that elicit inter-individual choices among group members has been more immediately useful. These techniques, feasible not only in small but also in middle-sized groups, help in identifying the informal structure of leadership or factions. They make possible the study of group properties such as authority, communication, cohesion, morale, or consensus at the level of the individual. These properties are important not only in explaining the behavior of individuals in groups, but also the actions of a group as a whole.

Through techniques of this kind, then, it is possible to broaden the range of political phenomena that can be made available to behavioral analysis and to refine and systematize political behavior research. However, this is not meant to minimize the difficulties in the way of subjecting political behavior to scientific inquiry. I think that the practitioners of the behavioral persuasion in politics are more sensitive to the problem of a science of politics than those who deny its possibility.

It does not seem very fruitful to specify what a behavioral science of politics might look like "in the end" because science is an ongoing endeavor that has no end. In general, the behavioral persuasion tries to develop rigorous research designs and to apply precise methods of analysis to political behavior problems. In its methodological orientation it is concerned with problems of experimental or *post facto* design, reliability of instruments, and criteria of validation, and other features of scientific procedure. Its function, as I see it, is to produce reliable propositions about politics by reducing error, which involves the invention of appropriate tactics of research, and by measuring error that remains through the application of relevant statistical techniques. As limited as the present success of the behavioral scientific enterprise in politics may be, the alternatives are even less satisfactory.

The discriminating feature of the behavioral persuasion in politics is, above all, its sensitivity to error in its observations of politics and its suspicion of *a priori*, formulated, universal "truths." It proceeds in terms of contingencies and probabilities, rather than in terms of certainties and verities. It represents an attitude of mind, a persuasion as I have called it, that takes nothing for granted and accepts as valid only the results of its inquiries when it would be unreasonable to assume that they can be explained solely by the operation of chance. This is a difficult standard to live by, perhaps more difficult in politics than in other fields of human action. For in politics as in physics and metaphysics, man looks for certainty, but must settle for probability.

BIBLIOGRAPHY

SELECTED STUDIES OF POLITICAL BEHAVIOR IN INSTITUTIONAL CONTEXTS

Campbell, Angus, Converse, Philip E., Miller, Warren E. and Stokes, Donald, *The American Voter*. (New York: Wiley, 1960.)

Dahl, Robert A., *Who Governs? Democracy and Power in an American City*. (New Haven: Yale University Press, 1961.)

Kaufman, Herbert, *The Forest Ranger: A Study in Administra-*

tive Behavior. (Baltimore: Johns Hopkins University Press, 1960.)

Key, V. O., Jr., *American State Politics.* (New York: Knopf, 1956.)

Lipset, Seymour M., Trow, Martin, and Coleman, James, *Union Democracy.* (New York: Free Press, 1956.)

Matthews, Donald R., *United States Senators and Their World.* (Chapel Hill: University of North Carolina Press, 1960.)

Schmidhauser, John R., *The Supreme Court: Its Politics, Personalities and Procedures.* (New York: Holt, Rinehart and Winston, 1960.)

INTERDISCIPLINARY FORMULATIONS OF POLITICAL BEHAVIOR

Dahl, Robert A., and Lindblom, Charles E., *Politics, Economics, and Welfare.* (New York: Harper, 1953.)

Lasswell, Harold D., *Power and Personality.* (New York: Norton, 1948.)

Leighton, Alexander, *The Governing of Men.* (Princeton: Princeton University Press, 1946.)

Snyder, Richard C., Bruck, Henry W., and Sapin, Burton, *Foreign Policy Decision Making.* (New York: Free Press, 1962.)

THEORETICAL STATEMENTS OF THE BEHAVIORAL PERSUASION

Dahl, Robert A., *A Preface to Democratic Theory.* (Chicago: University of Chicago Press, 1956.)

Easton, David, *The Political System.* (New York: Knopf, 1953.)

Lasswell, Harold D., and Kaplan, Abraham, *Power and Society.* (New Haven: Yale University Press, 1950.)

Mitchell, William, *The American Polity.* (New York: Free Press, 1962.)

APPLICATIONS OF BEHAVIORAL TECHNOLOGY IN RESEARCH ON POLITICS

Berelson, Bernard R., Lazarsfeld, Paul F., and McPhee, William N., *Voting: A Study of Opinion Formation in a Presidential Campaign.* (Chicago: University of Chicago Press, 1954.)

MacRae, Duncan, Jr., *Dimensions of Congressional Voting.* (Berkeley: University of California Press, 1958.)

Schubert, Glendon, *Quantitative Analysis of Judicial Behavior.* (New York: Free Press, 1959.)

Truman, David B., *The Congressional Party.* (New York: Wiley, 1959.)

Wahlke, John C., Eulau, Heinz, Buchanan, William, and Ferguson, Leroy C., *The Legislative System: Explorations in Legislative Behavior.* (New York: Wiley, 1962.)

CHAPTER TWO

❋ ❋

THE SOCIAL
MATRIX

Man's political behavior and relations are only part of his existence as a total human being, yet they are easily abstracted from the more comprehensive social environment. For some of the purposes of political analysis, this is both legitimate and necessary. Not all of man's manifold social relations are politically relevant, but enough are to suggest that we pay attention to the social matrix of of political behavior. Otherwise political description and explanation may be readily distorted or seriously misinterpreted. A person deeply involved in politics may be dealt with exclusively from the political point of view, or a person who is not involved very much may be treated as if he were totally alienated from the political arena. The elite and mass models of contemporary political society come close to making assumptions of this kind about political behavior. Neither image is likely to do justice to political reality. Political man, unlike some other models of man, is not an abstraction, but socially related to other men in a variety of ways that make him a total human being.

The analysis of political behavior can best proceed, therefore, by locating man as a political actor in the social matrix of interpersonal relations. The notion of a matrix implies that human behavior, including political action, consists of interactions and transactions that orient people towards each other, making them mutually responsive. I find the concept of "role" most useful to capture these relations, but it is the web of all of man's interpersonal relations, the social matrix, that gives behavior, including political behavior, its characteristic structure.

It is convenient to think of this structure in terms of a vertical and a horizontal dimension. The vertical dimension consists of man's group relations and can be analyzed in terms of the concept of "group" broadly interpreted to include all interpersonal collectivities. The horizontal dimension consists of those differentiating strata that define the upper and lower limits of either interpersonal or intergroup contacts. Role, group, and strata, then, will serve as conceptual building blocks of the social matrix.

ROLE AS A BASIC UNIT

In its simplest form, political behavior, like all social behavior, involves a relationship between at least two human beings. It is impossible to conceive of political behavior on the part of a person that does not have direct, indirect, or symbolic consequences for another person. The most suitable concept for analyzing a relationship between at least two actors and for determining the political relevance of the behavior characteristic of the relationship is "role," for we are not interested in all of a person's behavior but only in that aspect which is relevant to a political relationship.

The concept of role is familiar to most people. We

speak of the father's role, the teacher's role, the minister's role, the judge's role, and so on. What we mean in all of these instances is that a person is identified by his role and that, in interpersonal relations activating the role, he behaves, will behave, or should behave in certain ways. In looking at man's social behavior or judging it, we do so in a frame of reference in which his role is critical. If we do not know a person's role, his behavior appears to be enigmatic. But a child ringing a doorbell is unlikely to be mistaken for a political "doorbell ringer." Political behavior, then, is always conduct in the performance of a political role.

Out of observations as simple as these, social scientists have built a variety of theories about the origins, structure, functions, and meanings of social roles. Whatever its uses in everyday language or scientific research, role seems to commend itself as a basic unit of social and political analysis.

Role can be used as a conceptual tool on all three levels of behavioral analysis: the social, the cultural, and the personal. It is a concept generic to all the social sciences. On the social level, it invites inquiry into the structure of the interaction, connection, or bond that constitutes a relationship. On the cultural level, it calls attention to the norms, expectations, rights, and duties that sanction the maintenance of the relationship and attendant behavioral patterns. And on the personal level, it alerts research to the idiosyncratic definitions of the role held by different actors in the relationship. Role is clearly a concept consistent with the analytic objective of the behavioral sciences. It lays bare the *inter*-relatedness and *inter*-dependence of people.

On the social level, many of the most immediate interactions can be analyzed in terms of polar roles: husband implies wife; student implies teacher; priest implies communicant; leader implies follower; representative implies constituent, and so on. The behavior of one actor in the relationship is meaningful only insofar as it affects the behavior of the other actor or is in response to the other's behavior. Whatever other acts a representative may perform, for instance, only those in the performance of his constituent relationships are of immediate interest in political behavior analysis. I say of immediate interest because, in actuality, no single relationship is isolated from other social relationships in which the partners to the focal relationship are likely to be involved.

Many relationships are not structured by unipolar roles alone. In most cases, a role is at the core of several other roles, making for a network of roles that can be very complex. A legislator is "colleague" to his fellow legislators, "representative" to his constituents, "friend" (or "enemy") to lobbyists, "follower" to his party leaders, "informant" to the press, and so on. Whatever role is taken, simultaneously or seriatim, what emerges is a very intricate structure of relations in which one role is implicated in several other roles.

A role may be implicated in several networks. For example, the mayor of a city is not only a chief executive, a role that implicates him in several other role relationships related to his position, but he is also involved in many other relationships of more or less direct relevance to his political roles. He may be a husband and father, an alumnus of the local college, a member of the Rotary Club, a lawyer, a churchgoer, an investor in a local business, and so on. Depending on circumstances, these roles may complement each other, be mutually exclusive, or conflict. A network of roles reflects the complexity of social and political behavior patterns and warns against treating any one role as if it were exclusive.

Analytically, each network of roles can be thought of as a "role system." This has two corollaries. First, some roles are more directly related to each other than are other roles. For instance, the roles of husband and father or legislator and representative are intimately connected. Other roles may be less so. The existence and degree of their mutual implication is always subject to empirical determination. The legislator's role as a lawmaker is less likely to be related to his role as a parent than it is to his occupational role as, say, an insurance agent. This does not mean that the parent role is altogether irrelevant in his legislative behavior. A legislator with children attending public schools is probably more interested in school problems than a legislator who is a bachelor. The notion of role system directs attention to the totality of social behavior. At the same time, it points out the need of specifying the boundaries of the particular system under investigation.

The second corollary of role system implies that a change in one role may have consequences for the actor's other roles and, therefore, for the relationships in which he is involved by virtue of his roles. (This must not be confused with a change in position. When a Senator becomes President, his Senatorial role is terminated. His new position will make for new roles that greatly affect his other role relationships). As an example of role change, take the representative who finds it impossible to accept instructions from his constituents and increasingly relies on his own judgment. In the technical language of role analysis, this is a change from the "delegate" to the "trustee" role. It is likely that this change in the representational role will have consequences for the legislator's party-relevant roles. He might change from a partisan follower into an independent.

The structure of role relationships is not only patterned but also fluid. One source of change in role is a change in the expectations of others in the role system. Another source may be an actor's own redefinition of his role. These possibilities suggest the importance of treating role concepts from a cultural and personal standpoint as well as a social one.

On the cultural level, role refers to those expectations of a normative sort that actors in a relationship entertain concerning each other's behavior. These are the rights and duties that give both form and content to the relationship. A relationship can be maintained only as long as the participants are in agreement as to what each actor must or must not do in the performance of his role.

If there is disagreement over what kind of behavior should be expected, the relationship is likely to disintegrate.

Expectations which define roles and give direction to the behavior of actors in a role relationship are cultural in two ways. People do not continuously define and redefine their mutual relations and expectations. If a relationship had to be defined anew with each interaction, or if expectations had to be elaborated with every new encounter, stable social life would be impossible. In fact, most of the crucial role relationships are well defined. They are well defined because expectations are widely shared and transmitted through time. There is, then, a broad cultural consensus as to what the rights and duties pertaining to social roles are, and there is consensus on the sanctions available to participants in a relationship if behavior should violate agreed-on norms.

There may be more or less agreement from one role to another, from one culture to another. In Western culture, there is a broad consensus as to what kind of behavior the role of parent vis-à-vis the child calls for, though there are differences in role conceptions from one subculture to another. But if a role is located at the center of a network of roles, consensus on expectations is more difficult to identify. Only some minimum agreement might exist. For instance, it is difficult to say without inquiry just what behavior is expected of the politician. For the politician is involved in a multitude of relationships, with other politicians, community opinion leaders, financial patrons, spokesmen of interest groups, friends and neighbors, government bureaucrats, and so on. Each set of these others, themselves role-takers in the relationship, may have its own particular expectations as to how the politician should conduct himself. Consensus cannot be taken for granted.

Precisely because role expectations may be widely shared and relatively permanent, they give stability to the relationship. Role relationships thus make for stable patterns of behavior and minimize what would otherwise have to be considered arbitrary behavior. Understanding a role means that we know how a person should behave and what he should do in the performance of a role. This includes knowledge of probable sanctions and thus makes accurate prediction in social relations possible. This ability to predict another's behavior, always, of course, within the limits set by expectations and on the assumption that behavior will agree with the role, permits the partners in a role relationship to shape their own conduct in anticipation of the other's reactions. In some respects, this is a kind of guessing game without beginning or end. The repetitiveness of the game makes for patterns of behavior that produce those uniformities of behavior whose cultural-normative source is not especially felt (for more on this subject, see Chapter Three).

Role analysis aids in discriminating between norms for behavior and actual performance of a role. It may be argued that the best way to identify a man's role is to see how he actually behaves. A role, it would seem, is best reconstructed from performance. But this procedure, apparently so objective, ignores an important aspect of behavior, its meaning. The same bit of action may have different meanings for different actors (and, of course, different observers). Meanings are important in politics because politics is eminently concerned with the consequences of behavior. These consequences require evaluation. Roles as normative expectations of an actor himself concerning his conduct or of others provide meaningful criteria of evaluation that would otherwise remain quite arbitrary. For this reason, the distinction between the normative and behavioral components of a role is analytically and empirically necessary.

Even if there is a wide consensus on roles, there is always a good deal of variation in their performance. This may simply be due to the fact that a role is defined not only by others' expectations but also by an actor's own conception of his role. Admittedly no self-conception of a role can be completely different from the conceptions of others in the role relationship. In spite of differences in behavior, most conduct is recognized for what it is because roles can be identified. But though we may see ourselves as others see us and take appropriate roles, roles are never taken in identically similar ways. The explanation may be that two actors taking the same role may have somewhat different self-conceptions of the role because the others to whom they react are different actors with different expectations. This interpretation remains on the level of social and cultural analysis. And if the deviation is minor, socio-cultural analysis is sufficient. If it is major, it is necessary to find more personal clues.

Actors do bring idiosyncratic perceptions of the interpersonal situation, attitudes, and motivations to a role. Role analysis does not preclude, but may require, investigation of role conceptions from the point of view of the actor's personality. An actor's capacity to take certain roles is predicated on the possession of certain personality characteristics. Just what these are is a subtle problem of theory and research. I shall come back to it in the fourth chapter. But whatever hypotheses are formulated about personality in politics, they cannot ignore the wide range and the great variety of possible political roles. It would be quite erroneous to assume a one-to-one relationship between a political role and a given personality type, possibly treating personality as the independent and role as the dependent variable. This would deny the autonomy of analysis on the social level.

Role conflict may stem from various conditions, but two are noteworthy. These may actually be divergent expectations of a person's behavior. A city councilman may expect the city manager to guide and direct the council's legislative business, while another councilman may expect him to abstain from policy recommendations. Or there may be disagreement between others' expectations and an actor's own conceptions of his role. Moreover, the demands made from one role system to another may be so intense that behavior in the performance of various roles cannot satisfy role requirements. For example, involvement in the life of the Senate may so absorb a member's time that he cannot meet his obligations as a representative of his state. In all of these cases, role conflict is likely to have dysfunctional consequences of either a social or a personal sort. On the social level, certain functionally necessary roles may not be taken. For instance, conflicting expectations concerning the democratic politician's role may deprive a group of strong leadership. On the personal level, role conflict may so disorganize behavior that it becomes highly erratic, irregular, and even irrational.

Study of how role conflict is avoided or resolved suggests a number of possibilities. I shall only list them. First, some roles are more pervasive than others and conflict is resolved in their favor. Second, some roles are more clearly defined than others, which again aids the resolution of conflict in their favor. Third, some roles are more institutionalized than others, leaving the actor relatively little choice. Finally, roles are more or less segmentalized so that, depending on circumstances, even potentially conflicting roles can be taken.

THE VERTICAL DIMENSION—GROUPS

One might argue that "group" is an expendable concept. The argument would be that group is a loose, connotative term, impossible or at least difficult to define operationally, and what cannot be defined for measurement does not exist. What exists in reality is not a group but a pattern of interaction among people. Therefore, the concept of group is useless because it cannot tell us anything significant about reality.

The argument is fallacious. We cannot deny that, for certain purposes, individuals interacting with each other cannot be treated as empirically joint units, that is, as groups. And as a group, people can be treated analytically as interacting with other groups, even though, in reality, individuals rather than groups are involved in concrete relationships. Otherwise one could not speak meaningfully of inter-group, inter-governmental or inter-national relations.

This does not imply that in using group as an analytic concept, one is necessarily committed to one or another of the so-called group approaches or to particular methods of observation and measurement. Moreover, because we can think of groups as collective actors, it does not follow that group is necessarily the most useful analytic concept. But if the proof of the pudding is in the eating, the usefulness of any particular formulation of political behavior problems in group terms lies in the empirical results.

However, along with the vagueness of the concept, there is a problem in the enormous variety of groups that may be politically relevant. This does not represent an insuperable obstacle to the use of the concept. For it is possible through conceptual articulation to reduce the great number of concrete groups to manageable analytic proportions. Once we distinguish between group as a concrete structure and an analytic one, group, given its proper label, may prove useful. If concrete groups—family, neighborhood, party, organization, or whatever—are thought of as analytic structures such as primary or secondary groups, in-groups, or out-groups, formal or informal, reference or membership groups, two very practical results may be noted. First, retention of the concept of group with analytic labels attached reduces empirical complexity; and second, it permits generic considerations about diverse, concrete groups that would otherwise be difficult to entertain.

Attaching analytic labels to a concept is not the same thing as defining it. It has an orienting function. It directs the researcher's attention to what he wishes to investigate. It points to certain patterns of behavior to be described and explained, and it provides convenient, but only convenient, handles for doing so. If on inquiry, the label does not fit the facts, it can be abandoned. This procedure saves us from claiming too much or too little for analysis of political behavior in group terms. It does not say that all political behavior is group behavior, as some extreme group theorists would have it; nor does it suggest the opposite, that group analysis of political behavior is a dead end, as some anti-group theorists claim. It seems to me that a model of politics that ignores group altogether risks incompleteness.

But are role analysis and group analysis not mutually exclusive? The answer is "no." The advantage of conceiving of political behavior as conduct in the performance of political roles is that it concentrates not simply on the individual person alone, but simultaneously on those others in the person's social environment whose expectations contribute to his role-taking. These others may be other individuals, but they may also be groups. Now the role concept implies that if the others are a group, the group is not something outside of the role-taking individual. Just as the role concept refers to the existence of a relationship, so the concept of group refers to the particular character of the relationship. Though every group can be analyzed in terms of the roles that members (a role) take towards each other or towards non-members, not every role relationship can be analyzed in terms of group. Whether the latter is possible is a function of the properties of the relationship that must be discoverable as independent of the roles involved. If such properties can be identified and differentiated, and if analytic labels can be attached, group can be used as a meaningful unit of analysis not only in treating groups as political actors, but also in accounting for some of the roles taken by individual persons in the group and vis-à-vis other groups.

There is no intrinsic conflict between analysis of political behavior in terms of either role or group. Whether one wishes to employ one or the other concept is largely a question of the problem to be analyzed, a matter of theoretical preference or research strategy. For some purposes it is certainly sufficient and economical to think of political behavior almost exclusively in group terms. For instance, voting behavior can be and has been analyzed in this way. Group analysis of electoral behavior does not exhaust what one may want to know but, depending on the problem one poses, it may be superior to either role analysis or some other type of treatment. On the other hand, the study of legislative behavior is not likely to get very far without a more refined analysis of the roles that each legislator can take as the member of a legislative group. While his membership as such can tell us something about his legislative behavior in general, it is not likely to tell us very much. Analysis of the legislator's multiple roles may, or may not, lead us to the other groups to which he belongs, with which he identifies, or to which he refers in his legislative preformance.

The very vagueness of the concept of group forces the investigator to discriminate initially among the types of relationship in which he is interested. Clearly the relevance of a group in a person's political behavior is likely to vary with the character of the interaction. Of critical importance are the size of the group, its permanence, the degree of intimacy or formality in intra-group relations, the degree to which members identify with each other or group symbols (solidarity), the extent to which attributes or attitudes are shared (homogeneity), the group's tasks and the degree of specialization among the members, the formal system of coordination of individual activities, and so on. Depending on specification of these group properties, we can characterize groups as primary or secondary groups, associations, organizations, communities, factions, cliques, parties, and so on. Whatever the classification, political behavior is likely to vary with the type of group in which the individual is involved. As a result, a good deal can be said about his political behavior from knowledge of the type of groups that serves as a concept of analysis.

Group properties probably account not only for stability in political behavior but also for change. That the children from a Republican family may become Democrats, that friends who are no longer members of the same social circle may part political ways, that people long

politically apathetic may be activated by group influences, and so on, are empirical phenomena well enough
known. Changes in political behavior may be due to a
person's shifting from one group setting into another,
since new patterns of political behavior often follow new
group affiliations or identifications.

It would be folly to rely exclusively on knowledge of
a person's group affiliations to predict his behavior. While
the group is a factor to be reckoned with, it is only one
factor. If the individual's behavior itself is viewed as a
component of the group, we can avoid the rather
mechanistic notion of group influence on behavior. Instead of thinking in one-directional terms—the group's
influence *on* or *over* the individual—we can view the relationship between group and individual as reciprocal or
transactional. Indeed people may use political opinions or
behavior to gain entry into a group, to find new friends,
to make themselves at home in a new community. This
may involve conscious or unconscious behavior, and it
may or may not involve changes of belief. This kind of
anticipatory socialization is particularly frequent in political group membership. One's political views, whatever
their sources, may lead an individual to seek out groups
whose views he anticipates to be congenial to his own.

The group has at its disposal powerful sanctions in the
form of positive commandments or negative injunctions
to enforce conformity to group values, attitudes, and expectations. But we cannot assume that the individual is
simply the victim of forces he cannot resist and influence
in turn. Whatever patterns may be found in empirical reality, the group concept is neutral to the range of variations that may be characteristic of the relationship between individual and group in different group structures.

Groups range from the most casual and informal small
group to highly institutionalized and coercive organizations. If one adds the degree of political relevance that a
group may have for an individual's behavior, the task of
research appears formidable. Moreover, and paradoxi

cally, groups one might least expect to have political relevance are likely to be sources of lasting identifications, demands, and expectations in the political order. The pervasiveness of group-anchored aspects of political behavior has been demonstrated by research on such varied subjects as the family as an agency of political socialization, on peer groups as reservoirs of political recruitment, on neighborhoods as foci of political involvement, on communities as carriers of political values, on organizations as molders of political opinion, on nations as recipients of political loyalties, and so on.

Not the least important factor in determining the character of the individual-group relationship is the simultaneity of groups in the individual's social environment. Multiple group membership or overlapping group membership facilitates or impedes social integration on levels above and beyond the group itself. Multiple group membership interests us not only because of its consequences for individual political behavior, but also for the whole network of inter-group relations that constitutes the vertical dimension of the social matrix. An image of atomized groups, like the image of atomized individuals, is not a viable model of group analysis. The degree to which groups are in harmony or conflict or to which they co-exist without overt contact is largely a function of the number of overlapping memberships and the intensity of a person's relationship to different groups.

Of more immediate interest in the analysis of political behavior is the possibility that an individual's relationship to one group somehow affects his relationship to another group. If the attitudes, values or goals of the groups are harmonious, the individual's political behavior is surely affected in ways different from a situation in which they clash. In this case, the individual is likely to be subject to "cross-pressures." This is an unfortunate term because, once more, it connotes a kind of individual helplessness vis-à-vis the group. But whatever the expression, one individual-group relationship always seems to implicate another. The notion of "cross-pressure" suggests the need to disentangle often complex patterns of social and political relationships.

The possibility that group interests and loyalties may be at odds is also an important source of role conflict. These conflicts engendered by cross-pressures become most evident in critical situations where choices must be made and where latent contradictions, arising out of multiple group memberships not normally experienced, make behavior erratic. For instance, on an issue like censorship of a particular book or movie, a man's religious affiliation and commitment might well come into conflict with his membership in or identification with an organization devoted to civil liberties. Attention to the consequences of multiple group relationships on the level of the individual sensitizes the political analyst to a broad range of behavioral problems that otherwise remain hidden. Of course, many roles stemming from relationships with different groups need not conflict. And even if they do conflict, men may be only vaguely aware of the contradictions. It is not the fact of multiple group relationships, but its possible dysfunctional consequences for role-taking in situations where political decisions must be made, that is of special interest from the behavioral point of view.

A group's significance to a person is a psychological problem. If every person brings into the group relationship certain predispositions and attitudes, group analysis cannot be limited to group structure, processes, and goals, but must accommodate these individual psychological variables. Groups are objects of human experience making for different orientations. Perception of the group's relevance to an individual's personal needs and goals or one group's greater attractiveness as compared with other groups, and so on, are factors that, in turn, affect the relations among groups as collective actors. Considerations of this sort, stimulated by the concept of group on the individual level, may be a rich source of particular hypotheses about political behavior on the group level of analysis.

The group concept psychologically treated calls attention to certain symbolic associations that relate the individual to groups to which he does not belong. These groups seem to be particularly important in politics, where a great deal of behavior is only indirectly of an interactional kind. A person's goals, values, attitudes, and opinions may be derived from and shaped by identifications, perceptions, and comparisons which are not immediately traceable to his group memberships, but for which the existence of groups constitutes an environment of reference. The more generalized concepts of "reference group" and "reference group behavior" are potent explanatory tools of political analysis.

The orientations characteristic of reference group behavior may be affective, as in identification; cognitive, as in definitions of a situation; or evaluative, as in comparative judgment. Identification with a political party, a reform movement, or a persecuted minority may lead to a wide range of political action not explicable in terms of either a person's roles or group affiliations; yet the existence of groups in the individual's symbolic environment may be critical. Likewise an individual may explain political situations to himself by referring to the attitudes or opinions of groups he values. The reference group becomes a source of perceptions and standards, definitional or normative, that affect political behavior. Finally, reference groups can serve the individual as a frame of comparison for evaluating himself and others. Comparing his own circumstances with those of others, a city resident who pays high tax rates may move into an unincorporated suburban neighborhood with low tax rates. These distinctions between affective, cognitive, or evaluative reference group functions are, of course, only analytic. In reality, reference groups may serve all three functions simultaneously.

In a political world removed from one's own direct experience, what one perceives as real or significant is likely to vary from one group context to another. Groups provide the individual with those definitions of the situation without which behavior, in politics as elsewhere, would be highly arbitrary. Seeing one's own political opinions and values shared by others will validate political reality. This is probably true of the person only occasionally concerned with politics, and even more so of the person continuously involved—the politician, the party worker, the legislator, the judge, the bureaucrat, and so on. Group "belongingness" or reference group orientations not only reinforce a person's political perceptions and beliefs, but they also tend to shield him from political experiences which he might find unpleasant. It is a common observation that we read only what we wish to read, or that we avoid contact with people with whom we might disagree.

A great deal of research has shown that, especially in perceptually ambiguous situations, group-anchored attitudes are projected onto situations that, in reality, are quite different from what they are perceived to be. Reference group analysis does not pretend to explain why some groups rather than others are chosen as foci of orientations. It seems likely that this choice is related to the second dimension in terms of which political behavior in the social matrix can be analyzed, the horizontal ordering or stratification of human relationships.

THE HORIZONTAL DIMENSION—STRATA

In politics and out, people do not interact with each other beyond an identifiable range of relationships. Even within a group, if it is large enough, some members rarely meet or have direct contact with other members. This is partly due to different persons performing functionally differentiated roles that do not require direct relations. In part, the roles are differently evaluated and inter-action between the incumbents of such roles is not considered desirable. Or, if interaction does occur, what the in-cumbents of functionally differentiated and differently evaluated roles should or should not do—their rights and obligations—is more or less strictly regulated, for example, in a military organization or a feudalistic social formation. But even in as intimate and small a group as the nuclear family, the parents (and sometimes even the husband vis-à-vis his wife) and children are set off from each other in clearly discernible ways. Similarly in the huge group formations we usually call societies, certain individuals or groups are differentiated from others, thus creating a system of relationships that would in all likelihood not exist if functional or valuational differentiation were absent.

Just as the concept of group alerts one to the vertical pattern of social relations, so the concept of stratum calls attention to the horizontal levels of the social matrix within which individual and group relations take place. The notion that political behavior and social relations are generally stratified is, of course, one of the oldest, most central, and persistent organizing ideas of political and social thought. Built around it one finds numerous and diverse concepts such as formulations of caste, class, or status, in short, formulations of social structure as the horizontal dimension of the social matrix. The concept of stratum seems to me analytically and empirically more serviceable because it is valuationally neutral and does not commit the analyst of political behavior to a particular theory that might seek to account for the sources of stratification, and its effects on political behavior and the whole system of relations in which people are involved.

To think of social or political relations, whether inter-individual or inter-group, as stratified means that behavior is bounded by upper and lower limits beyond which it does not extend. In general, status refers to inter-individual and class to inter-group differentiation, though these concepts have no stable and unambiguous empirical referents on which observers might be agreed. The distinction between status and class as a distinction between individual and group referents seems to be useful in looking at a functionally very complex matrix such as that of the United States. Here incumbents of high status positions in groups of relatively low class character may yet interact with their opposites in groups of high class character.

For instance, labor union leaders interact with industrial managers more often than with their own rank and file. The example suggests the utility of the concept of stratum. Evidently a new stratum, the "higher servants" of labor, business, or government, that is neither a status group nor a class in the conventional uses of these terms, has emerged as a result of such differentiation and collaboration.

Whether one thinks in terms of status or class, then, the limits imposed on behavior, including political behavior, by a person's or group's location in a stratum of the social matrix may be more or less rigid or flexible, depending largely on the total number of horizontal levels that can be identified. Within any horizontal order, whether characterized in terms of class or status, individuals or groups in neighboring strata are more likely to come into contact with each other than individuals or groups in widely separated strata. In a highly stratified system with many levels of status differentiation, there is little contact between incumbents of status positions that are removed from each other by more than two or three steps. On the other hand, in a small entrepreneur-manager type of system with few intervening levels, the boss is in continuous contact with all employees, even if they occupy different status positions.

The same is likely to be the case in the larger social order characterized by classes. In the United States as a whole, classes are difficult to identify, though most observers speak of a middle class and a working class, or of white and blue collar classes. Due to lack of sharp differentiation, there is a great deal of interaction across these class lines and class is less likely to be a critical factor in political behavior than in societies with more highly stratified social orders. Where class stratification produces many levels, there is more interaction within than between classes and political behavior takes on a more pervasive class character.

The determination of any system of stratification is an empirical question guided by theoretical speculations about relevant criteria of differentiation. The notion of stratification is grounded in the assumption that patterns of behavior in the performance of social roles, within or without particular groups to which people belong, are socially evaluated. This assumption is shared by most theorists concerned with stratification, though they disagree on the criteria of evaluation, the character of the ensuing horizontal structure, the rigidity or permeability of strata boundaries and, last but not least, the problem of *whose* evaluations should supply relevant criteria of stratification. Who is to say whether and what kind of system of stratification exists in the social matrix?

In general, two approaches to stratification pervade the bulky body of writings on the topic. For better or worse, they are called objective and subjective approaches. According to the objectivists, the existence of status or class strata and the order of stratification—what is high and what is low—are immanent in the social order and quite independent of the feelings, attitudes, or perceptions that people may have concerning them. It is the task of the observer, using whatever objective indices his theoretical propositions suggest, to stratify a population. He may do so, as Marx did, by locating a person in terms of his position vis-à-vis the relations of production or, as some modern social scientists do, by applying such criteria as income, education, or occupation. Although people objectively located in a stratum are assumed to share a "consciousness of kind," certain "interests," or other subjective feelings, these aspects are considered dependent variables that cannot be used in ascertaining the system of stratification. Indeed they are to be explained by stratification independently and objectively arrived at.

The subjectivists, on the other hand, start with the assumption that precisely because social evaluation accompanies every functionally differentiated relationship, those in the horizontal order are themselves best qualified to supply criteria of stratification. Again the criteria are thought to be immanent. The observer is only supposed to find out just how people appraise either their own or others' location in the social order. Various methods have been used to discover the subjective meanings that people give to their class or status, but they need not concern us here. Controversy over the validity and reliability of stratum indicators, objective or subjective, has been acrimonious. Again this is not the place to go into the merits of this controversy. Whatever method is chosen, the critical issue is the utility of the notion of stratification as a handle for analyzing political behavior in the social matrix.

This issue can only be clarified through empirical research. The usefulness of any method of stratification depends on its ability to predict consequences for political behavior that may be traced to a person's location in the horizontal dimension of the social matrix. One of these predictions might relate to an individual's choice of the groups with whom he identifies or to whom he refers in his political conduct.

It must be remembered that stratification is only one of the many variables in terms of which differences in political behavior may be explained. Any hypothesis that seeks to explain a particular pattern of political conduct is always circumscribed by several other variables. As stratification involves some valuation, a group's set of values is always necessarily relevant. On the societal level, class systems in two nations may appear to be very similar from a structural perspective, yet the valuational meanings given to both class and politics may be quite different. As a result, political behavior related to stratification in the two nations may differ a great deal. For instance, recruitment practices into the political elite may vary. Civil servants might be largely recruited from the upper social stratum in one system; in another, they might be recruited from the lower strata. In the first system, public service might be looked on as an obligation; in the second, as a sinecure to be exploited for personal advantage.

For reasons such as these, hypotheses about the consequences of stratification for political behavior are unlikely to be universally valid. The general proposition that stratification and political behavior are significantly related is probably viable only to the extent that analysis is contextual. Just what particular patterns of political behavior will be found in any social matrix analyzed in terms of stratification cannot be predicted from the structural characteristics of the matrix alone.

Insofar as politics is purposive activity through which a group—whether a national society at one end of the matrix or the nuclear family at the other end—engages in collective decision-making, it is generally considered to have the attributes of self-consciousness as a group and interest. Both of these are very vague concepts. But we assume that, whatever the particular system of stratification, the existence of strata makes for self-consciousness and the specification of interests. The degree to which this is so is always a matter of empirical determination. The notion that a stratum, whether a class or status group, develops consciousness of kind stems from the observation that it is a necessary correlate of interaction. People in constant contact with each other but cut off from others are likely to see themselves as being the same and to see the world around them in similar perspective. They are also likely to view their interests in similar ways and they will behave in politically like ways to advance these interests. Out of speculations such as these Marx built his theory of class consciousness, class interest, and class conflict. But whether stratification makes, in fact, for consciousness of kind and common interests and, therefore, for similar patterns of political behavior, cannot be taken for granted. It must always be subjected to empirical testing.

Much in the relationship between stratification and political behavior depends on the extent to which a given social order is open or closed, that is, the extent to which it permits or prohibits, facilitates or impedes social mobility. The rigidity or flexibility of a stratification system is a function of many factors, ranging from material conditions to customary practices and ideological perspectives. The relatively high degree of social mobility in the United States for both individuals and groups has impeded the development of class consciousness, at least in the Marxian sense, and made politics relatively free of class considerations, but only relatively so when compared with societies where stratification is more rigid and pervasive. This is only another way of saying that, compared with other systems, stratification is less relevant in the United States in explaining variance in political behavior.

It does not mean that class is irrelevant in American politics. A great deal of research on voting behavior, pressure politics, community politics, and recruitment practices shows that stratification may have more to do with politics than the American ideology of mobility and equality led earlier observers to suspect. On the other hand, the same studies show that it is relatively easy for individuals or groups in American society to identify with the values and symbols of the elite, even if they cannot actually change their place in the order of things. Such identification across strata boundaries makes for limited awareness of class interests in a collective sense, with obvious consequences for political behavior.

BIBLIOGRAPHY

ROLE ANALYSIS

Gross, Neal, Mason, Ward S., and McEachern, Alexander W., *Explorations in Role Analysis*. (New York: Wiley, 1958.)

Nadel, S. F., *The Theory of Social Structure*. (New York: Free Press, 1957.)

Wahlke, John C., Eulau, Heinz, Buchanan, William, and Ferguson, LeRoy C., *The Legislative System: Explorations in Legislative Behavior*. (New York: Wiley, 1962.)

Wilensky, Harold L., *Intellectuals in Labor Unions: Organizational Pressures on Professional Roles.* (New York: Free Press, 1956.)

GROUP ANALYSIS

Bentley, Arthur F., *The Process of Government, A Study of Social Pressures.* (Chicago: University of Chicago Press, 1908.)

Golembiewski, Robert T., *The Small Group: An Analysis of Research Concepts and Operations.* (Chicago: University of Chicago Press, 1962.)

Katz, Elihu, and Lazarsfeld, Paul F., *Personal Influence.* (New York: Free Press, 1955.)

Olmstead, Michael S., *The Small Group.* (New York: Random House, 1959.)

Truman, David B., *The Governmental Process: Political Interests and Public Opinion.* (New York: Knopf, 1951.)

Verba, Sidney, *Small Groups and Political Behavior: A Study of Leadership.* (Princeton: Princeton University Press, 1961.)

STRATUM ANALYSIS

Barber, Bernard, *Social Stratification.* (New York: Harcourt, Brace, 1957.)

Centers, Richard, *The Psychology of Social Classes.* (Princeton: Princeton University Press, 1949.)

Eulau, Heinz, *Class and Party in the Eisenhower Years.* (New York: Free Press, 1962.)

Janowitz, Morris, *The Professional Soldier.* (New York: Free Press, 1960.)

Marvick, Dwaine (ed.), *Political Decision-makers: Recruitment and Performance.* (New York: Free Press, 1961.)

Namier, Sir Lewis, *The Structure of Politics at the Accession of George III.* (New York: St. Martin's Press, 1957.)

CHAPTER THREE

❁ ❁

THE CULTURAL
CONTEXT

Like the air we breathe, culture, however defined, is so close, so natural, so much a part of what we are that we are not aware of it. We notice it only when we move from one culture into another. The most important aspect of culture is that its existence is predicated on the existence of another culture. One culture always constitutes the environment for another. Only awareness of different cultures sensitizes us to the culture in which we live, act, think, feel, and judge. Otherwise we are culture bound—we do not know who we are nor why.

Culture is all pervasive. It permeates, without our awareness, every aspect of our daily living. Political behavior is no exception. We cannot fully understand it unless we treat it culturally and locate it in the wider cultural context. This enables us to see how our own political behavior is similar to or different from political behavior in another culture. The ideal of scientific objectivity requires cultural analysis of political behavior, if for no other reason.

The difficulty of analyzing political behavior in terms of culture is that our language and language-related modes of thought, themselves products of culture, stand in the way. We say that culture *is* this or that, or that it *does* this or that; but culture is not a thing nor can it act. It does not exist outside or apart from behavior as something that can be identified independently of behavior or the results thereof, regardless of whether these results are symbolic or material. Culture is a mental construct abstracted from the behavior of people and their works. Despite this, it is possible to speak of *a* culture because, as I suggested, it makes sense to speak about culture only if we can specify the existence of more than one culture.

At the risk of ambiguity, I shall continue to use the term "culture" without defining it for the simple reason that, among the host of over 250 available definitions, I know of none that is neither too narrow nor too inclusive. Ambiguity is not necessarily a drawback here. As a concept, culture is a synthetic rather than an analytic construct, and I wish to use it to stimulate investigation, not to conduct it. In an essay of this sort, conceptual refinement may be more of a handicap than an advantage.

More important when looking at political behavior in cultural terms, we are still observing the same behavior that we observe when we use social terms. It is not the behavior involved that is different but our observational standpoint. We are simply moving to another level of analysis. Just as the notion of social matrix and related concepts are useful in viewing politics in social terms, so the notion of cultural context and related concepts call our attention to the cultural environment of politics and to politics as a cultural phenomenon itself.

CULTURAL PATTERNS

We speak of culture patterns when we observe similarities in the behavior of people in the same culture that are relevant to diverse, functional aspects of social action. Though their religious, economic, military, or political practices serve quite different functions in a group's* existence, the patterns of behavior involved may be very similar. For instance, authoritarian patterns of behavior may be characteristic of different functional areas of a group's life: child rearing, religious practices, economic organization, or political decision-making. If we observe similar patterns that are pervasive and stable through time (or, if they change, do so gradually), we can assume, at least for working purposes, that they are not due to chance. We attribute the similarities in behavioral patterns that are functionally specialized to the working of culture.

Suppose we ask why so many people in the United States are relatively uninvolved in politics? The question invites us to compare political behavior in this country with political behavior elsewhere. But we need not necessarily make such a comparison in order to look at American political behavior in cultural terms. Even without it, the concept of culture suggests that the patterns evident in mass political behavior may also be present in other functional areas of social behavior.

We may try initially to strengthen our observation. It impresses us that political interest and involvement rise rapidly as an election approaches, but fall off even more rapidly thereafter. Moreover, the interest seems to be more like a spectator's than an active participant's. The idea of spectator interest makes us look for other functional areas where spectatorship seems to be the typical response pattern.

It has often been suggested that American politics has the characteristics of a game. Indeed, a perceptive journalist once called it "the great American game." The analogy itself is a cultural artifact, and our language sup-

---

* I am using "group" in the most generic sense of the term as referring to a society, a nation, a region, a community, a tribe, an organization, a social class, a committee—any collectivity whose members are in more or less direct and permanent contact with each other.

ports it. Like baseball or any other game, politics is "played." It is played by "rules of the game" that must be observed and professionals play the best game. Admiration for a job well done and emphasis on winning are part of the general behavioral pattern. We cheer the victor, forget the loser. Those who also ran are the forgotten men of American public life. The game, in sports as in politics, is partly for entertainment. The spectator pattern of American mass behavior, mirrored in the language of sport, is a pervasive feature of the culture. (Notice, too, that we "watch" the stock market and "play" it.)

Admittedly, these are speculations based on the most superficial kinds of observations. I have introduced them only to illustrate that behavior is likely to be patterned in more or less consistent ways in different functional areas of life within the same culture. This notion, in turn, leads us to view behavior as an integrated whole rather than a set of disparate items. This does not mean that different functional aspects of behavior are necessarily related; they may be quite disconnected. Politics and economics may or may not interpenetrate. Politics and leisure may or may not be related. Yet even if not connected structurally, the same or similar cultural patterns will pervade different functional areas. Discovery and analysis of these patterns is, of course, only a first step in the cultural analysis of human behavior.

To avoid any misunderstanding, I am not saying that all behavior within a group that shares a culture is characterized by identical patterns. It is not. The concept of culture merely suggests that viewing behavior as a whole may help in explaining particular items of behavior. Moreover, there are enormous difficulties in employing cultural analysis as we move from relatively small, functionally undifferentiated, simple groups, such as preliterate societies or even an adolescent urban gang, to complex, functionally highly differentiated modern collectivities.

Although some sweeping and ingenious characterizations have been made of American culture in all its heterogeneity, they are little more than impressionistic. The analysis of complex cultures involves many theoretical and methodological difficulties. But this is not an argument against the use of the concept of culture in modern settings. In the first place, if discontinuities in behavioral patterns outweigh the continuities, this is itself a cultural datum to be taken into account in the analysis of political behavior in a complex, cultural context. And second, the very useful concept of subculture is predicated on the assumption of the existence of a common culture. This common culture may prove to be empirically elusive, leading to the kind of impressionistic analysis that has been made of American culture, but its existence must be assumed nevertheless. The technical difficulty of discovering cultural patterns in diverse areas of behavior must not be confused with the absence of patterns.

The culture concept puts the accent on wholeness, which guards us against taking behavior in a functional arena—be it sports, religion, the economy, or the polity—out of its cultural context. The failures of attempts to transfer political institutions from one culture to another are well known. In these cases, behavioral patterns could not adjust or be adjusted to externally imposed arrangements. Similarly, within a group it is risky to view political institutions and processes outside of the cultural context in which they are embedded. *How* individuals behave in functionally different areas of activity is likely to be more continuous than *what* they do. For this reason, the variance in the political behavior of different groups may be illuminated by information about their behavioral patterns in other functional activities, that is, by cross-cultural comparison of similarities and differences. At least it will help us avoid making generalizations about political behavior, whether parochial or universal in scope, that are necessarily culture-bound.

The pervasiveness of cultural patterns from one functional area of life to another, from politics to economics, from economics to crime, from crime to sports, and so on, suggests that cultural analysis may be particularly useful in understanding public policies and the manipulative aspects of political behavior. All too often, social problems in the real world, graft and corruption, apathy and resistance to reform, social justice and peace, and so on, are seen as if they were soluble only on the political level of action. Cultural analysis suggests that these problems may be deeply rooted in a group's total way of life, and that their solution requires more than treating them by political means. Often these political remedies are themselves so rigidly prescribed by cultural do's and don't's that they must remain ineffective. Cultural analysis can serve as a potent diagnostic tool of political behavior, diagnosis being preliminary to prognosis and political therapy.

We speak of cultural patterns of behavior when they are widely shared, rather than social or personal patterns. The degree to which they must be shared before we can say that they are is an interesting question. I have never encountered a very satisfactory answer. Knowledge of the extent to which cultural patterns pervade different functional areas is of interest in defining the boundaries of a culture. But it is unlikely that in a world of close intercultural contacts the boundaries can be clearly specified. Patterns weave across cultural boundaries, causing similarities in behavioral patterns. As a result, the question of how much sharing is necessary for us to speak of cultural patterns remains moot.

More critical in appraising the cultural factor in political behavior is the degree of stability in the patterns. This stability of behavioral patterns is probably the most telling evidence of the working of culture in politics. Moreover, the rate of change that can be observed in behavioral patterns is itself a cultural phenomenon. Here, too, we are facing subtle technical problems. The rate of change may reach a point where it is hardly permissible to speak of patterns of behavior at all. What this point is, I cannot say. In any case, increasing randomness in behavior suggests cultural crisis and possibly cultural transformation. From this point of view, political institutions are cultural products par excellence. For by definition, an institution is a set of widely shared, regularized patterns of behavior that are fairly stable through time. Institutions are, of course, only the most overt aspects of cultural patterns in political behavior. Covert patterns are equally crucial components of a political culture.

In general, then, we can speak of cultural patterns in political behavior if the patterns are similar to other patterns in a group's way of life, if they are widely shared and change only slowly. How these patterns have come about and how they are transmitted are questions of considerable interest to the cultural analyst of political behavior. The most plausible hypothesis is that they are the cumulative results of learning, and that they are transmitted from generation to generation in the process of socialization. The patterns are a group's adaptations to the environment in which it lives, and they change as new generations are forced to adapt to changing environmental conditions, including cultural changes in the environment of other cultures. The more cultural contact there is, the more cultural patterns are likely to change. Political behavior research is increasingly concerned with the processes of political socialization and the consequences of socialization for the maintenance of political institutions and the more informal patterns of political conduct.

CULTURAL ORIENTATIONS

I have suggested so far that we can look at patterns of political and other behavior as outside observers who infer uniformities and regularities from what they see. If *we* name the patterns, as I have when speaking of an authoritarian pattern or a game pattern, the procedure is altogether arbitrary. Our observations as outsiders are, of course, cultural products also—in the case of the scientific observer of the culture of science. The critical characteristic of the scientific culture is its cognitive intersubjectivity: that is, the agreement among scientists that the observed phenomena are, in fact, what they are alleged to be. To make this agreement possible, science has developed its own patterns of behavior, its rules of method. Presumably if these rules are adhered to, the same observations will be made and, more important, the same inferences will be drawn from the observations. We say that the methods of observation, the observations themselves, and the inferences from the observations have meaning.

Likewise, the patterns of behavior in other functional areas of life at the core of cultural analysis have meanings to people themselves. These meanings enable people to understand each other's behavior and coordinate their conduct. Political behavior, as all other human behavior, has not only form and content but also meaning for the actors who play the game of politics. If political behavior were observed only in terms of its content and patterns, the observations so obtained would be very partial and misleading. Political behavior, though similarly patterned, may have quite different meanings to the actors whose behavior is observed. Much traditional political inquiry has been purely formal in the sense that it was limited to the observation of patterns and took the meaning content of behavior for granted. Political institutions or constitutions were described and their formal similarities and differences were noted, but what these patterns meant to the people involved was not investigated. Rather meanings were ascribed, usually on the basis of the observer's own cultural understandings.

Cultural analysis of political behavior cannot be limited to objective observation of patterns. It is concerned with the meanings that people give to these patterns, regardless of whether they are formally institutionalized or not, including the functions that they see as being served by politics. Such analysis is impossible unless the individual person, as bearer of cultural meanings, is the unit of analysis. In highly literate and articulate cultures, the meanings given to politics can be studied by analyzing documentary evidence. Content analysis now serves as a useful tool of inquiry into verbal symbols and their manifest as well as latent meanings. But there are difficulties. Documentary materials may not be sufficiently explicit to permit the discovery of meanings. And they may be neither typical nor representative, but rather parataxic, more indicative of the writer's idiosyncratic interpretations than of widely held cultural understanding.

The meanings people give to their behavior may be highly conscious, subconscious, or unconscious. They may be so sacred they forbid articulation, or they may be highly secular and profane. Whether they are one or the other or in between is likely to depend on a culture group's exposure to other cultures. The more isolated a group, the more ingrained and traditional its behavioral patterns are likely to be and the more unconscious the meanings given these patterns. At the other extreme, groups in close cultural contact are likely to be highly conscious of the meanings they attribute to their own behavioral patterns and those of their cultural neighbors. Homogeneous groups take their patterns for granted; heterogeneous groups are forever in search of meanings that give their behavior symbolic significance.

Behavioral analysis of politics cannot afford to ignore the meanings that people give their own behavior because these meanings have consequences for their own political actions and those of others. Meanings are the organizing principles of behavior through which people make themselves at home in the world and orient themselves to action, including political action. If, like behavioral patterns, meanings are widely shared and relatively stable, it is possible to construct a group's cultural self-image. How people orient themselves to the groups to which they belong and those to which they do not belong gives meaning to their behavior. Indeed *social* behavior is impossible without the existence of widely shared, stable, and agreed-on meanings that serve as a frame of reference in conduct. Meaning, figuratively speaking, is the glue that binds people together in groups and divides them from others.

In general, cultural analysis of political behavior can easily discriminate between various types of meanings in terms of a group's orientations to political action. Some of these orientations are cognitive. These are a group's perceptions of reality in terms of which it defines its environment. Such perceptions can range from highly scientific and sophisticated concepts at one extreme to the most superstitious and irrational notions about reality at the other, from scientific knowledge to the most primitive beliefs. How people behave in politics, how they make those collective decisions that guarantee their survival as a group, is powerfully influenced by their image of the world they live in.

Differences in image from one culture to another are potent determinants of political conduct. Whether the environment is seen as friendly or hostile, whether expectations about the future are optimistic or fatalistic, whether group demands are pathologically exaggerated or minimized, orientations of this sort are critical frames of reference for political behavior. The reason for such differences is of central interest to the cultural analyst. However they may have come about, political behavior research must treat them as potentially important explanatory variables. The belief that man can shape his world through his own efforts will lead to a different kind of political action than the view of man at the mercy of forces over which he has no control. A culture group whose time perspective is in the past may find it difficult to cope with the present, just as a group whose perspective is largely in the present may be unable to plan wisely for the future.

Orientations to political action are also affective. Here we deal with those widely shared emotional responses to which we give names like loyalty or morale. These emotions may be positive or negative, and they may be directed in different degrees towards different objects.

Whether man relates himself to others in terms of what is conventionally called love or hate, trust or fear, is likely to have significant consequences for his political behavior. Insofar as one or another of these orientations is widely shared and more or less accentuated in a given culture makes an enormous difference in politics. It will produce notions about other political actors, whether individuals or groups, as friends or enemies, as objects of identification or withdrawal. Whether politics is experienced as a life-and-death struggle for existence, as a competitive though friendly game, or as a cooperative enterprise for mutual aid, is likely to be a function of widespread affective components in the culture.

Finally orientations to political action are normative. Included here are the evaluative standards by which judgments are made about political behavior, the ethical rules that guide behavior, as well as the goals considered worthy of attainment. Some of these orientations may be actually operative ideals whose observance is not in doubt. Others may be ideal standards that differ from what people actually do when they guide or evaluate their own and others' conduct. In politics, the degree of agreement on ideal patterns of conduct is probably an important stabilizing and legitimizing factor in actual behavior. Conflict between ideal patterns and operative ideals becomes a central source of political tensions that call for solutions. Behavioral norms and values, whether ideal or operative, are crucial items on the behavioral agenda of inquiry into politics.

Just as meanings are implicit in patterns of political behavior, and transmitted by the members of a group, so are cognitive, affective and normative orientations. Insofar as meanings and orientations constitute a more or less coherent and integrated set of symbolic expressions, they come to be accepted as self-evident systems of belief.

By belief I mean the non-logical, pre-rational components of the total cultural ideology. Belief in this sense is not rooted in reasoning and direct observation, and it is highly resistant to disproof. Belief can only be given up in exchange for another belief. Beliefs are the self-evident propositions that everybody knows to be true without need for further proof. Putting these propositions in doubt arouses hostility, causes pressure for conformity, or leads to excommunication in rigid cultural contexts. From the cultural point of view, the analytical problem is not whether beliefs can, in fact, be tested by the methods of social science or at least dissected by the criteria of logic. Cultural orientations to action differ in the degree to which their components can or cannot meet the requirements of proof or logic. Rather the point is that propositions of this order are believed because they are widely shared, relatively stable, and successively transmitted and, in turn, give direction to social and political action.

Belief systems are characteristic of even highly sophisticated and secularized cultures. That one's own form of government is far superior to any other; that only a particular economic system can guarantee a high standard of living; that war is rooted in human nature and cannot be prevented; that one group is out to destroy another, these are some of the beliefs more or less widely shared at one time or another, even in cultures that take pride in rational conduct. Often these beliefs have only symbolic functions with few consequences for actual political action. But under certain conditions, for instance in crisis situations when the group's survival is at stake, beliefs have an important effect on the political order. In the American South, the belief that Negroes are impulsive, childlike, overemotional, short on intelligence and initiative, docile, easily frightened, or incredibly superstitious has been the most pervasive single factor in political behavior. That this belief in "white supremacy" is neither rational nor subject to disproof does not negate its effectiveness in giving meanings to political orientations as well as actions.

Analysis of political culture is not concerned, then, with the truth of beliefs but with the functions they perform. Precisely because beliefs are grounded in emotion rather than logic and because they are experienced as certainties rather than probabilities, orientations to political action grounded in a total system of belief that defies disproof have a strong influence on political cohesion. Belief systems serve to give people a sense of mutual identification, to protect them against doubts and the dangers, real or imaginary, of an environment that must be controlled. For this reason, threats to belief systems arouse the most passionate and violent types of reaction. They are considered as equally necessary to the survival of the individual as of the group. There is generally a discrepancy between the degree of sacredness with which belief systems are invested and the realistic functions that the systems and their component orientations may perform as integrating or disorganizing elements in the total cultural configuration of political behavior.

CULTURAL CHANGES

Apart from socialization, the sharing of political beliefs and norms within a culture is due to those pressures towards conformity stemming from man's relatedness to man. This interdependence gives rise to expectations that become cultural norms, though at first they may be only statistical regularities. The pressures to conform, then, are not somehow external to behavior but characteristically cultural components of behavior. In politics, these pressures are greatly accentuated by coercive sanctions purposefully designed to assure survival of the community, institution, organization, or small group. But the cultural perspective also warns us against overestimating the coerciveness of political power. The more traditional analysis of politics as a power phenomenon overlooked the pressures towards conformity that are cultural and, therefore, are not experienced as coercive. To be a loyal citizen, a faithful partisan, a conscientious taxpayer, and so on, are cultural expectations. We act as we do because we have learned to do so without questioning it. If our actions were widely questioned, requiring enforcement by loyalty oaths and other types of coercive assurance, the political culture would likely be in crisis.

Emphasis on the pervasiveness of cultural factors in political behavior must not be thought of as cultural determinism. More often than not, a deterministic interpretation of politics, as of other human pursuits, is due to a fallacious distinction between culture as a kind of thing and individual behavior. This fallacy leads to the notion of culture as an independent force, governed by its own inner laws in the face of which man is helpless.

On the contrary, since culture and all that the concept implies—structural patterns, functional actions, meanings, beliefs, norms—are abstracted from the behavior of man, they are surely subject to change by man. If culture is manmade rather than "natural," the individual is free to change it. Whether he will probably depends on the degree to which cultural patterns, beliefs, and norms satisfy man's needs and the adjustments he has to make vis-à-vis the natural environment. It is only when cultural patterns and meanings become rigid that they turn out to be obstacles to change needed in the face of new developments. We call this cultural lag. Political behavior patterns and institutions are particularly subject to cultural lag because they are sanctified by customs and traditions. Patterns of political behavior are difficult to break. All the same, the cultural perspective in the study of political behavior is of value not only to the political scientist for whom it provides contextual relevance, but also to the policy-maker who is constantly concerned with orienting behavior in the direction of preferred group goals.

Culture is not a conceptual strait jacket. Cultural phenomena are only one set of factors affecting political behavior. Choice, in politics as in economics or in private decisions, though circumscribed by what is socially possible and culturally permissible (and, I might add, individually acceptable), is ever present. The reason for this is simple enough: cultural patterns, meanings, or norms, though widely shared, are rarely transmitted in an absolutely uniform manner. This is, of course, truer of complex groups than simple ones. In general, freedom of choice in behavior is likely to be greater the more complex the group's web of social relations. But in complex groups with many subcultures where individuals rarely share the same set of interpersonal relations, each person tends to be exposed quite differently to a great variety of cultural and subcultural cues that, in their particular combinations, make for a more or less unique behavioral expression.

Moreover, the cultural stimuli impinging on man in the course of socialization into new experiences are quite inconsistent particularly in complex, modern groups. Apart from contributing to the individual's freedom of choice, these inconsistencies are also sources of cultural transformation. As a result, culture is in a state of continual change. The rate of change differs from culture to culture, in turn affecting social patterns and relations. The changes themselves arise out of cultural inconsistencies, conflicts of norms between subcultures and contacts with alien cultures. Political cultures are subject to the same transformations. The transformations may be rapid or slow, depending on the cultural configuration as a whole, the requirements of social and political interactions, and individual preferences. In turn, politics in modern secularized groups may itself become an element of either integration or decomposition in the culture as a whole.

Culture, including political culture, is dynamic. This is best observed when a new group comes into existence. Whenever a group is formed, whenever individuals come into effective contact with each other, the members of the group face similar problems of mutual adjustment to each other and to non-members. It is difficult to imagine, of course, that already available cultural solutions will not be taken from the larger culture. But the group would probably not have formed in the first place if all sought after solutions were already embodied in the group's cultural model. In other words, the group's behavior in search of itself is not as yet consensually validated. Behavior in such a culturally emerging group is tentative and exploratory. Mutual identifications and commitments to group goals are at first limited. Only gradually, as the members come to know each other, will rules emerge for dealing with the problems that brought the group into existence and for regulating the group's conduct. Analysis of the formation of groups can give us much insight into the dynamics of political culture.

When culture is conceived of as emergent, our attention is called to the time dimension of political behavior. Although most political behavior research is conducted in the present and often lacks historical depth, cultural analysis cannot avoid noting the genesis and development of political patterns and beliefs in different eras. In tracing the emergence and evolution of traditional patterns, the political behaviorist is developmentally rather than historically oriented. He is not interested in past occurrences for their own sake. Rather he tries to trace and possibly explain how present patterns of political behavior have come to be what they are. Developmental reconstruction is difficult. Dead men do not talk and heavy reliance must be placed on documentary evidence that may not be representative of relevant past patterns. If regularity in political behavior is to be more than an assumption, long-range as well as short-range trends must be investigated, both to give time-dimensional depth to analysis and to make comparison possible across continuous periods of time. Because cultural change is relatively slow, the analysis of political culture patterns and their transformation aids in pinpointing those more rapid shifts in individual or group behavior that result from purposive, political and social action. Political action, in turn, is likely to have an impact on the more general culture. The active intervention of the American Federal government in Southern affairs, for instance, has decisive and determinable consequences not only for the politics of the South, but for Southern culture in general.

Cultural analysis is necessarily comparative, even if

comparison is not made intentionally. Deliberate comparison only articulates—an important "only," of course —what otherwise remains latent and, as a result, may cause misleading inferences. From the comparative standpoint, the discovery of similarities must logically precede the specification of differences. It is only against the background of similarities that differences can be observed. This is a point of method especially difficult to abide by in the study of politics. For politics, almost by definition, commits the observer to the specification and clarification of differences rather than similarities. The conflictive aspects of politics point up how persons or groups involved in a political relationship differ, not how they are alike in characteristics or goals.

Looking at politics in cultural terms is a compensatory remedy. If two things are to be compared, even though, as in politics, their differences seem blatant, it is necessary to assume a *tertium comparationis*, some hypothetical notion, more or less explicit, of just what it is that is to be compared. This third element, a purely hypothetical construct, must contain aspects common to both things being compared. Without this assumption of commonness, comparison is impossible. If cultural analysis is undertaken self-consciously with comparison in mind, it leads to the discovery of similarities as a necessary condition for seeing differences.

These considerations are in line with the conventional assumption of behavioral science that uniformities can be identified in the conduct of individuals and in the functioning of institutions, and that these uniformities are due to common human and social factors which transcend cultures. The fact that all groups have some form of decision-making structure through which collective problems can be solved is more significant than the fact that the governing function is performed in one group by a council of elders, in another group by an autocrat, or in a third group by an assembly of all adults. But treatment of a particular institution does not take us very far if analysis is limited to the discovery of similarities in functions performed by different structures. This makes cultural analysis all the more useful as a tool of political inquiry: it always assumes that between different groups—states, tribes, parties, households or other decision-making collectivities—there are also likely to be differences in political behavior patterns, beliefs, or norms that are culturally conditioned and, therefore, fully understandable only within the particular cultural context in which they are embedded. In this regard, then, cultural analysis is both a requisite of and corrective for comparative political inquiry.

POLITICAL CULTURE

The concept of a political culture is something of a paradox. I have argued that cultural analysis cannot successfully focus on a particular functional area of a group's total way of life without simultaneously focussing on other areas. Yet the concept of political culture seems to limit our attention to those patterns of behavior and those orientations that, presumably, characterize only one aspect of a group's existence. Such a self-imposed setting of boundaries would seem to make it impossible to specify and measure the salience of politics within the larger culture and the consequences of different political patterns and orientations on the culture as a whole. But the task of analysis is to delineate the degree to which a culture is politicized. As the concept of political culture would seem to imply, a partial cultural analysis is really untenable if one accepts fully the premises of method from which cultural inquiry proceeds.

But cultural analysis, like all scientific inquiry, always involves a process of theoretical abstraction and empirical isolation. The concept of political culture does not deny that the political culture is embedded in a larger culture. In short, it must be interpreted to refer to a subculture, and it is only for convenience sake that we do not speak of political subculture (as we should) or political sub-subculture (as we might). A subculture, the notion suggests, shares certain patterns and orientations with the larger culture from which it is analytically (but certainly not empirically) set off by other patterns that are *relatively* unique to itself. There may even be a conflict of patterns between the political subculture and the more general culture. For instance, the hierarchical patterns of military behavior may conflict with egalitarian patterns in the general culture. Indeed, observable tensions in the American military establishment may be traced to conflict between the military subculture and the general culture. Sacred orientations in the political culture, like its fetishes, may conflict with the generally secularized views of the culture as a whole. Resulting tensions on the cultural level of analysis may be mirrored on the social and personal levels, thus yielding further insights into individual and inter-individual behavior.

Cultural analysis of political behavior seems more viable in a group (using the term in its most generic sense to refer to an institution, a local community, a social class, a religious order, a geographical region, an age group, and so on) than in the larger societal contexts where it is usually employed. In fact, within the United States, for instance, fruitful subcultural analyses of political behavior have been made in groups as diverse as the Senate, a small village community, a slum area of a metropolitan city, the military establishment, a democratic trade union, an old-age movement, a Japanese relocation center, and many other political groups or settings. Though all of these groups share the larger culture, each exhibits its own patterns of behavior, including political ones. And there are subcultures within subcultures as there are groups within groups. Even the smallest social unit—the nuclear family, the clique, the work team, the committee—has its own culture. In most respects a dual cultural function is performed in these groups: the group transmits not only its own peculiar ways of thinking and doing things, but also serves as a kind of conveyor for transmitting the more general cultural patterns.

The existence of political subcultures in particular political situations, whether formally institutionalized or not, is always an empirical question. It cannot be prejudged. But the notion of subculture as the more general concept of culture alerts the analyst of political behavior to the possibility that otherwise non-explicable variances in political action may stem from subcultural differences. In a country like the United States with its high degree of social intercourse and mobility, both vertically in the group order and horizontally in the stratification order, there is a great deal of cultural homogeneity among subcultures. Differences in political behavior due to subcultural differences may be difficult to observe. But on close scrutiny, subcultural political contrasts will not escape the behavioral microscope. Indeed, any empirical construct of the American political culture will have to be built on minute, subcultural analyses of political behavior.

Political culture, then, refers to the patterns that can be inferred from the political behavior of groups as well as the beliefs, guiding principles, purposes, and values that the individuals in a group, whatever its size, hold in common. Each individual, of course, has his own conception of the political culture that influences what he does or does not do politically. For this reason, cultural analysis alone, just as social analysis alone, does not exhaust what is to be discovered about political behavior. Full analysis must also take account of the personal basis of political conduct. But to the extent that individual patterns and meanings more or less coincide, the concept of culture and all it implies is a useful handle of political behavior research.

In this sense, political culture refers to the consensus of numerous individuals, but a consensus that need not be precisely duplicated in any one person. On empirical research grounds, it is a concept probably more useful than "constitution" in defining a group's political working agreements. Political scientists have long sought to over-overcome the formal-legal definitions of constitution by speaking of the living constitution. This biological metaphor is more confusing than clarifying. The formal constitution of a polity is a record and a source of the behavioral patterns and norms that are components of the political culture. From the behavioral point of view, it is too restrictive to assume that a concept like living constitution can approximate the richness of patterns, beliefs, and orientations that guide political behavior in government and out. Political culture may as yet be an ambiguous concept, but it has the virtue of stimulating political behavior research along cross-cultural lines, within a major culture as well as between subcultures, which the notion of living constitution does not.

Although culture may itself not be an operational tool in a technical sense, it can, if properly constructed in a specific empirical context, aid in predicting political behavior with a high degree of probability. Of course, all depends on the accuracy with which any concrete political culture has been formulated by the investigator. A particular culture construct admittedly distorts reality in order to capture reality. The uniformities and regularities it posits are necessarily statistical, even though the procedure used in formulating the image of the culture is anything but statistical. The construct of a particular political culture or subculture is always a summary expression of many individual behavioral patterns. Most people within a group are likely to have some experience with many of the same patterns, though all may not be exposed to all the prevailing patterns. In the study of political behavior within a single culture, widely shared patterns can, therefore, be considered as constants, providing a base line for examining particular individual responses to particular political situations. On the other hand, in cross-cultural analysis of political behavior, differences in observed patterns and orientations are critical variables for studying responses in functionally similar political situations. In either case, cultural analysis permits the investigator to transcend the boundaries of his own culture.

BIBLIOGRAPHY

CULTURAL ANALYSIS

Linton, Ralph, *The Cultural Background of Personality*. (London: Routledge and Kegan Paul, 1947.)

Potter, David M., *People of Plenty*. (Chicago: University of Chicago Press, 1954.)

Redfield, Robert, *The Little Community*, and *Peasant Society and Culture*. (Chicago: University of Chicago Press Phoenix Books, 1960.)

Thompson, Laura, *Culture in Crisis*. (New York: Harper, 1950.)

VALUE ANALYSIS

Benedict, Ruth, *Patterns of Culture*. (New York: Houghton Mifflin, 1934.)

de Grazia, Sebastian, *The Political Community: A Study of Anomie*. (Chicago: University of Chicago Press, 1948.)

Morris, Charles, *Varieties of Human Value*. (Chicago: University of Chicago Press, 1956.)

Stouffer, Samuel A., *Communism, Conformity, and Civil Liberties*. (New York: Doubleday, 1955.)

CROSS-CULTURAL ANALYSIS

Almond, Gabriel A., and Coleman, James D., *The Politics of the Developing Areas*. (Princeton: Princeton University Press, 1960.)

Deutsch, Karl W., *Nationalism and Social Communication*. (New York: Wiley, 1953.)

Lipset, Seymour M., *Political Man*. (Garden City, N.Y.: Doubleday, 1960.)

Pye, Lucian W., *Politics, Personality, and Nation Building*. (New Haven: Yale University Press, 1962.)

SUBCULTURAL ANALYSIS

Banfield, Edward C., *The Moral Basis of a Backward Society*. (New York: Free Press, 1958.)

Vidich, Arthur J., and Bensman, Joseph, *Small Town in Mass Society*. (Princeton: Princeton University Press, 1958.)

Warner, W. Lloyd, and associates, *Democracy in Jonesville*. (New York: Harper, 1949.)

Whyte, William Foote, *Street Corner Society*. (Chicago: University of Chicago Press, 1943.)

Wood, Robert C., *Suburbia: Its People and Their Politics*. (Boston: Houghton Mifflin, 1959.)

❊ ❊

CHAPTER FOUR

THE PERSONAL
BASIS

The analysis of political behavior should be exhausted once man's social relations and cultural milieu have been accounted for. There would seem to be no room for looking at it on a personal basis. Indeed even if one knew nothing about a man's personality, a great deal of his political behavior could be satisfactorily explained in social or cultural terms alone. But throughout the history of political speculation from the Greeks to the present, there has always been the realization, however vague or mistaken in detail, that a politics which does not consider human nature can only be a very partial politics.

But to say that a man's personality has something to do with his political behavior is not saying very much. It only states an assumption: that what kind of personality a man brings to politics makes a difference. More relevant are these questions: when is it feasible and worthwhile to study political behavior from the point of view of personality? what can personality study contribute to the analysis of political behavior? These questions make the assumption that differences in political behavior are due to personality differences somewhat problematical. Personality may or may not make a difference. The problem, then, is to specify the boundaries of the functioning of personality in politics. It appears that the boundaries may vary a good deal, from problem to problem and situation to situation.

If we speak, as we do, of the effect of personality on political behavior, we are presumably concerned with the relationship between two variables. This formulation is not an altogether happy one. Personality, like culture, is an abstraction from behavior, not something independent of behavior. It is not directly accessible to empirical observation. Rather it is abstracted from and constructed out of the very patterns of behavior and feeling, past and present, that it is intended to explain and interpret. In speaking of the effect of personality on political behavior or of the relationship between them, we are once more using conceptual shorthand. I prefer to speak of the personal basis of political behavior because it suggests a distinction between those aspects of political behavior that are personal and those that are social or cultural. It is the relationship between the personal aspects on the one hand and the social or cultural aspects on the other that is the heart of the matter.

PERSONALITY IN POLITICS

"Of what use to a man is his political behavior?" the psychologist is likely to ask. In other words, the psychologist treats personality as the object of inquiry. Man's political behavior may interest the psychologist, when it interests him at all, because it is empirical grist for his theoretical mill. Hopefully, something called personality comes out of the mill. Depending on the psychologist's theory, man behaves as he does politically because his behavior satisfies personal needs, demands, and drives, or because it releases tensions and frustrations, or because it compensates for deprivations, or because it reveals private perceptions and values.

This way of looking at political behavior can tell us a great deal about the quality of political participation, the intensity of political preferences, or the individual's orientation to political action. But that personality expresses itself in the *political* arena is of only incidental interest to the psychologist. Insofar as he is concerned with the functioning of personality in social or institutional contexts at all, other arenas such as business, sports, or the arts can serve his purposes equally well, perhaps even better because they are more readily accessible to psychological investigation. Whatever the arena, therefore, the psychologist's basic question remains the same: of what use to a man is his economic behavior, his athletic behavior, or his artistic behavior? The behavior itself is assumed to be shaped directly by the needs, drives, predispositions, or fears and hopes of the individual actor. The arena has no existence independent of the psychological processes of the participants. Political behavior, or any other type of behavior, is conceived of as springing directly from personality.

For the political scientist, on the other hand, the functioning of the political arena as a behavioral system is the critical problem to be explained. His approach is necessarily different. He does not ask about the consequences of political behavior for a man's personality. Rather, he wants to know about the consequences of differences in personality for the performance of political roles and the working of political institutions. The personal meanings and motivations, conscious or unconscious, underlying a man's political participation or political preferences are of analytic interest because their discovery may contribute to an explanation of the political as a behavioral system. This system, it should be recalled, is always a network of interpersonal behavior. Analysis of the personal basis of political behavior can tell us, first of all, how and why a particular political actor relates himself to others as he does.

Moreover, if it can be shown that political activity serves a person to overcome a low estimate of himself, that it serves him to remove feelings of isolation and loneliness by making for personal involvement, or that political preferences are expressions of rebelliousness against or submissiveness to authority, and so on, the information may be of inestimable value in appraising the quality or durability of a political system. In the aggregate, knowledge of the personal basis of political behavior may illuminate the style of a political system, its adaptability to environmental conditions, its ability to satisfy human needs, and so on.

But political behavior is also responsive to requirements arising out of the interpersonal situation and to more or less widely shared goals, values, and expectations. Conformity to these situational requirements and cultural expectations will depend, in part, on an individual's capacity to respond, a capacity not unrelated to his personality. It also hinges on social and cultural sanctions, broadly interpreted as including both indulgences and deprivations more or less consciously perceived and experienced as guide lines in political behavior. Regardless of their personal motivations and predispositions, people tend to behave in more or less regular and predictable fashion, in politics and out. And their expectations concerning their own conduct and that of others are relatively stable and uniform. Some may be more conscientious in what they do, more enthusiastic, more eager to please, or more ambitious than others. However, despite such differences that undoubtedly stem from differences in personality, political processes and institutions function in ways quite unrelated to variations in personality. For instance, the policies and activities of a public welfare department are affected by more factors than the personality of its chief or case workers. The legally prescribed functions of the department, the professional ethics of social workers, the realistic assessment of client needs, the availability of financial resources, the traditions of the community, and so on, all of these factors are likely to affect the department's policies and activities.

The problem is to decide just when to deal with political behavior from the standpoint of its personal basis and how to do it. It is a subtle problem because we cannot talk about everything at once. One solution would be to argue, as has been argued, that in the end only personality matters, that only if man is unmasked, so to speak, can his political behavior be significantly explained. This argument is patently untenable because, as I have suggested, political processes and institutions function quite independently of variations in personality. Another solution would be to treat the personal basis as a residue, something to be investigated only after analysis on the social and cultural levels has yielded whatever is sought.

The problem is more complicated, for a number of reasons. But one reason stands out: unless we subscribe to an exclusively individualistic psychology, we must assume that what is social, cultural, and personal in political behavior is so intertwined that either over- or under-emphasis of any one distorts political reality. It does not follow, of course, that each political act, sequence of acts, or system of political behavior must always be treated on all three levels. These are not competing but alternate ways of looking at the same behavior. They may set limits to each other, but they need not conflict. The personal basis of political behavior cannot be treated in *a priori* fashion as either an exclusive or a residual level of behavioral analysis.

One might explore research strategies in two ways. First, one might look at the conceptual linkage of the social, cultural, and personal dimensions of political behavior. To what extent and how do alternate types of analysis complement or limit each other? Determination of the limits may suggest what particular level of analysis is most appropriate for whatever theoretical problem is to be solved. The second strategy is specifying the theoretical problem. One need not assume that all problems of political behavior require equally intense study of the personal basis, but one may assume that, in the present stage of scientific development, many problems may be equally well solved in social or cultural terms.

OPINIONS AND ATTITUDES

Political behavior research can be conducted on a broad front. At one end, there is the biographical study of outstanding individuals, statesmen, warlords, revolutionaries, and so on, as well as the man on the street (though one may question just what intensive analysis of the man on the street as an individual would contribute to an understanding of the political system). At the other end, the emotional reactions of whole nations, especially in times of crisis, or the aspirations and behavior patterns of mass movements are of intrinsic interest. Between these extremes, the political behavior of small groups (families, committees, juries), of politically attentive publics (politicians, opinion leaders, journal readers), of demographic aggregates (small businessmen, senior citizens, women), of organized collectivities (labor unions, farm organizations, utilities), or of institutionalized groups (legislatures, bureaucracies, military formations) is a matter of inquiry. Because the individual is the basic empirical unit of political behavior analysis, the very practical question arises whether it is feasible, in an economic and effective sense, to study the political conduct of nations, mass movements, large organizations, institutionalized groups, demographic aggregates and even relatively small groups in terms of their participants' personalities.

It sounds banal to say that the greater the number of individuals involved in a political system, the less sense it makes to seek full data concerning the personal basis of political behavior. It clearly is impossible to subject an adequate random sample of a national population or of a large group like an army to the same kind of intensive personality study that is possible in the case of individual political biography. This need not mean that survey analysis of the political behavior of large groups or aggregates, even of national societies, cannot benefit from theoretical formulations of personality. But in general, the kinds of problems which interest the political scientist, involving not only individuals as individuals but also more or less complex collectivities, though possibly psychological in formulation, do not readily lend themselves to analysis as problems of personality.

So far I have intentionally shied away from defining personality. It is difficult to use concepts referring to the personal basis without becoming entangled, wittingly or not, in some particular theory of personality. Almost every relevant psychological concept is invariably tied to some particular school of psychology or given different meanings by different schools. There would be no point in reviewing various definitions of personality here or adopting one of them. This is not a plea for conceptual fuzziness or eclecticism. It only means that since political behavior analysis is concerned with the individual as the empirical but not necessarily the theoretical unit of inquiry, it is advisable to avoid committing it to a particular theory of personality. For in the end such theory may not be strategically appropriate for the kind of problem to be solved.

The problem at hand is the best guide to the choice of approach. However personality is defined, in studying the personal basis we may deal with unconscious motivations and thought processes, including fantasies; with more or less visible reaction patterns (mechanisms of defense or cognitive dissonance); or with attitudes, perceptions, and preferences, rational or not, that can be more readily verbalized and discovered. Just how these aspects of personality are related to each other, just what emphases are to be given one or the other in constructing personality, just what techniques are best suited to producing the necessary data, and so on, are matters of immediate concern to the psychologist. They need not occupy us here. Our objective is not to formulate *homo politicus,* if this is possible, but to suggest strategies of research on the personal basis of political behavior in connection with quite diverse problems of politics.

In sum, analysis of political behavior in its personal aspects need not proceed from a theoretically consistent and integrated conception of personality. It may select those aspects that seem relevant to the problem and fit the population to be investigated to them. Research tools, as they are dictated by the size of the sample, and conceptual tools, as they are dictated by the problem at hand, are likely to influence each other. Formulations of political behavior in a large sample survey, which involves relatively short interviews with a population of considerable heterogeneity, must be necessarily limited to inquiry in terms of rather superficial perceptual or attitudinal questions. That these attitudes or perceptions may be anchored in interpersonal relations rather than the personality is beside the point. They may reveal some personal meanings that the individual gives his political activity.

The extent to which the researcher may draw inferences from such data on the functioning of personality in politics is a matter of scientific conscience. One may wish to interpret scaled responses to a handful of questionnaire items as indicative of an authoritarian *personality,* an anomic *character,* a tough-minded *attitude,* or simply a *feeling* of efficacy. Indeed this has been done, but there is the danger of over-interpreting this kind of data. The cold fact is that a certain number of people have responded in certain ways to a few questions. The pattern of an individual's responses may be suggestive, though it may or may not be evidence of personality in politics.

On the other hand, if one's research deals with a single individual or a few people, the personal basis of political behavior can be fruitfully explored through a prolonged interview of the Freudian tradition or, where interviewing is impossible, by exhaustive analysis of documentary data. In these cases, political behavior analysis will employ the intricate set of concepts from one or another theory of personality. This will undoubtedly yield a rich harvest of knowledge about the relationship between personality and politics. For instance, the interpretation of Hitler as a hysterical-paranoid personality may be set against the background of social and economic conditions in Germany and the emotional state of the German masses, providing insight into the dynamics of large political systems under certain conditions of stress and strain.

Only very few political scientists have ventured into this type of intensive personality research. This is due partly to strategic difficulties inherent in the research situation, partly to the fact that few possess the skill and training necessary for deep analysis. Of these two obstacles, I think the former is more critical. Living persons of political consequence are unlikely to submit to intensive study. In the case of historical figures, the nature and reliability of documentary materials is always open to question.

Somewhere between survey analysis and depth analysis, efforts are made to combine intensive, though not prolonged, interviews with projective tests, standardized personality inventories, and other procedures. These techniques are well suited to inquiry into political behavior because they are more widely applicable than deep analysis, yet more thorough than survey research can afford to be. They would seem to be especially useful in the study of small institutions, though so far they have been employed only in the study of small aggregates of isolated individuals. These techniques require a measure of diagnostic skills, too, but political scientists could learn them.

Depending on the strategy employed then, different conceptual aspects of personality can be selected for investigation of the personal basis of political behavior without commitment to some overarching conception of personality in politics. A comprehensive model of political man may be more of an obstacle than an aid. We may yet gain a good deal of insight into the personal basis of political behavior by examining those cognitive processes and affective orientations through which the individual seeks to cope with political life, including the situations and expectations that define his political roles.

The study of attitudes and perceptions is more immediately useful in discovering how political behavior affects large-scale political processes and systems than the kind of intensive inquiry that seeks explanation in terms of unconscious drives or other adaptive mechanisms of the psyche. Knowledge of how man perceives himself as a political actor, how he interprets the world of politics, how he values what he sees, and how he acts politically in pursuit of personal values can tell us a great deal about his political behavior.

Overt behavior, including opinions, can be revealing in several respects. Most obviously, perhaps, it can tell us something about government and politics as objects of perceptions and attitudes. Does the world of politics enter a man's perceptual field at all? Is the legislator aware of the interest groups in his environment? Are political campaign issues important to the voter? Once we establish perceptual relevance, we may investigate affective components of political attitudes. Does the legislator feel that pressure groups are helpful or harmful? Does the voter consider government as benign or evil, political candidates as attractive or not, political issues as urgent or not? Answers to these simple questions can tell us a great deal about a person's ability to differentiate, the values in terms of which he appraises reality, and his time perspectives. If not all pressure groups are perceived as powerful, which ones are and which ones not? What degree of influence is attributed to these groups? What criteria of judgment are applied? It is likely that the values involved in political judgments or the perceptions of urgency that reveal the political time perspective constitute a more or less patterned hierarchy, as well as a more or less permanent syndrome of political predispositions.

While different levels of the personal basis of political behavior are probably interrelated, one need not assume a one-to-one correspondence. A great many varieties of behavior or opinion may be rooted in common personality characteristics at the deep level of analysis, but the political behavior of diverse personalities may be identical. For instance, distrust of authority may express itself in unconventional political opinions or radical behavior *or* in compulsive demands for a just and powerful leader. Deep-felt dependency needs may underlie an ideology that glorifies obedience or one that insists on freedom. For this reason, we should always take care in interpreting opinions and attitudes, even if they seem to constitute a consistent pattern that suggests a personality syndrome.

VALUES AND PERSONALITY

From the research point of view, the conceptual plasticity of formulations about the personal basis of political behavior can be an operational blessing. It permits the psychologist to construct his model of personality by selecting from many aspects those that seem most fruitful in explaining a particular political behavior problem. Most psychological theories of personality consider typical mental states, drives, or mechanisms—whatever the nomenclature—as the most basic determinants of behavior. They consider perceptions, attitudes, or values as more or less peripheral layers of personality. But there is no intrinsic objection to choosing those elements of personality that seem most useful for a special problem of political behavior. I have already mentioned the advantage of paying special attention to perceptions and attitudes in the study of political behavior. It is also worthwhile to pay close attention to a person's values, whether he holds them consciously or not.

Values can serve as central organizing principles in studying the personal basis of political behavior. Presumably a person's values are sufficiently structured to constitute a value system; and if they do, the value system may well be the most stable component of political behavior. Therefore it is a critical task of research to discover the content of a person's value system, its arrangement and degree of internal consistency, and its relation to the culture that patterns the politics of the group to which the individual belongs. More than any other aspect of personality, personality-rooted values express the personal basis of political behavior.

To conduct this type of analysis, it is necessary to differentiate as sharply as possible between the personal and the cultural components in an individual's scheme of values. The culturally transmitted set of values is validated by being widely shared, though we can only discover it through studying the values of individuals. On the other hand, the value system of an individual, though transmitted culturally, should be more or less identifiable as unique in his political behavior. Unless the distinction is made, political behavior analysis is likely to be trapped in what I would call the fallacy of cultural correlation: that is, the error of inferring a personal value from a cultural value system. I believe that this error is made by those who substitute some pseudo-concept of political character for political behavior analysis. I have in mind those broad characterizations of social and political behavior that are so popular because they are so flippant: the organization man, the inside-dopester, or the status-seeker. Just because a culture like America's can be characterized in terms of the high value given personal success, individual mobility, or competitive achievement, it does not follow that these are the main values or even the sole values that shape the political behavior of particular individuals. In the first place, there are other values that are culturally transmitted and widely shared. And second, without empirical investigation in each case, we cannot tell in what combinations these values occur to constitute individual value systems. In fact, it is the special task of research to discover how widely shared and personally held values can shape a system that gives the individual's political behavior its relative stability and consistency.

Whatever the degree of political involvement, culture

determines significant aspects of an individual's personality. It does this not only in the form of role expectations and other behavior norms, as well as perceptual cues that orient the individual to his social and material environment, but also in the form of values. The individual internalizes these values in the course of socialization. They thus become aspects of his personality. Personalities in a given culture group can probably be characterized in terms of values held in common because the socialization process itself is culturally patterned. But as there are also discontinuities in a culture, and as socialization practices vary a great deal from subculture to subculture, values are transmitted and internalized in varying combinations and degrees of intensity, depending on an individual's peculiar circumstances. As a result, one individual's value system is rarely identical to another's, though enough similarities may exist to permit their description in terms of types. A personal value system, then, is not simply a replica of a cultural value system. Otherwise it would be impossible to account, on the personal basis, for the great variety in political behavior within the same culture.

Because values and value systems differ from one cultural context to another and from one person to another, problems of political relevance on the personal basis of behavior may be quite differently experienced and evaluated in different milieus. In particular, the way in which personal life experiences affect political behavior in the performance of roles is likely to depend on the culture's value system and, accordingly, the values given to personal experiences and correlate behavioral manifestations.

This may be illustrated by the possibly different consequences in different value contexts of primary identification as part of the socialization process. In most cultures, children find their identity through identification with the parent of the same sex in a particular phase of the growth process. The degree of success achieved in identification must be appraised against the background of culturally approved solutions. Now identification in

the primary circle interests us from the standpoint of political behavior because it seems to entail an individual's
responses to authority. The kind of identification
achieved with the father as an authority figure seems to
be of consequence for the kind of identification with later
symbols of authority—individuals like teachers, job
superiors, or political leaders, or groups such as community, institution, or nation.

Identification seems to have two main types of consequences for political behavior: submissiveness to or
rebelliousness against authority. However a culture's
value system will emphasize these possible types of response differently. In a culture that highly values authority as a set of expectations defining adult relationships, it
is likely that the process of identification in the nuclear
family will tend to polarize the alternatives of submis-
sion and rebellion toward more extreme solutions. On
the other hand, in a culture that places relatively low
value on authority, the working out of child-parent identification is less likely to have extreme solutions. In turn,
because the individual repeats the patterns experienced
in different stages of growth, primary identification and
resultant solutions tend to reinforce cultural values. But
as normality in behavior is defined culturally rather than
personally, individuals do not necessarily experience a
system of authority relations, whatever its shape, as either
especially indulgent or deprivational.

As a result, authority relations in some political systems
engender a great deal of submissiveness or assertiveness
without negatively affecting the system's stability, while
in some other system, comparatively lax authority relations also fail to affect adversely political stability. It
seems that in either case, differential evaluations of authority are sufficiently internalized to become strong
organizing principles at the personal basis of political behavior.

There is always an area of exploration for locating the
personal aspects of political behavior in the context of
cultural expectations. In other words, it is important to

determine just how a person's personal perspective—his more or less conscious identifications, demands and values—correspond to those consensually validated interpretations that are the "givens" of social conduct. For instance, if giving or withholding affection in childhood has differential consequences for behavior in maturity, empirical analysis has yet to determine just how affective orientations experienced early in life are interpreted in the cultural context. Discipline has different meanings in different cultures and subcultures. In a culture where severe disciplining is not only widely practiced but also approved, its consequences are likely to be different from those in a culture where stern discipline is restricted and disapproved. But just what these consequences are can never be left to deductive inference; they must be empirically verified.

For this reason, we should distrust attempts at characterological interpretations of whole nations in terms of some pervasive set of personality attributes inferred from the nature of socialization. Although national character is a widely used term, it is not a meaningful empirical concept. Many of the constructions of national character that have been made are largely intuitive and often based on casual observations, literary statements, or case analyses of limited scope. If they are based on large opinion or attitude surveys, the surveys may tell us something about the distribution of attributes in a population, but we should be even more suspicious of inferences about a hypothetical, if not mythical, national character.

Anthropological researches in small, simple societies have stimulated so-called national character studies. In small societies, model traits can possibly be explained by the exposure and limiting of children to a very narrow range of experiences that are constantly reinforced by a relatively homogeneous cultural value system. Early acquired characteristics at the personal basis of behavior may be important for the functioning of the social system. But we cannot assume that this happens in an equally simple way in complex, modern systems. I doubt that a given political structure, let us say democracy, is predicated on the existence of a democratic character, whatever that may mean. Of course, psychologically healthy people are preferable to unhealthy people in any system. But definitions of mental health are difficult to come by. Equating mental health with democratic predispositions only symptomizes a cultural myopia, pleasant and self-congratulatory as it may be.

ROLE AND PERSONALITY

The investigation of specific roles rather than broad patterns of conduct provides the most tangible evidence of the importance of the personal basis of political behavior. This follows from our initial acceptance of role as the basic theoretical unit of behavioral analysis.

We can think of role as that aspect of personality that refers to an individual's social identity. If this is so, research on political behavior must deal with the agreement between political roles as aspects of personality and other aspects. One may approach this problem from either end of the relationship. A psychologist, I would think, would be interested in learning how harmony or conflict among several concurrent role requirements affects the degree to which the personality is capable of modifying itself in response to particular role requirements. He would want to know how the relationship between role and other aspects of personality varies with the special characteristics of the individual. He would try to discover the degree to which a role is central or peripheral to a person's private needs and demands.

On the other hand, if role is the starting point of analysis, somewhat different concerns come into focus. No assumption needs to be made about the direction of the relationship—whether other aspects of personality shape role or are shaped by it. Nor is it necessary to assume either a zero or a one-to-one relationship. The degree of congruence between role and other aspects of personality is likely to vary a good deal.

The complexity of a political system is one cause of this. The more complex a system, the greater the number and variety of political roles. The sheer number of available roles and their heterogeneity are likely to reduce congruence between role and requisite personality characteristics. In a democracy like the United States, there are millions of citizens who participate in public decision-making by voting in elections. Hundreds of thousands engage in other forms of political activity. Thousands of others fill a great range of elective and appointive offices, in government or political organizations. People with quite different personality characteristics can function effectively in this sort of political system with its great variety of political roles. Only in the upper tiers of the political structure are personality characteristics more likely to be relevant in recruiting personnel for particular roles and in shaping the performance of these roles. But even in connection with these roles the democratic quality of the political system is likely to reduce the degree of congruence between role and other facets of personality.

For example, take an elective official like the American legislator. The number of simultaneously available roles is large because the legislator is implicated in a great number of interpersonal relationships. All of those he deals with—constituents, lobbyists, party leaders, administrators, colleagues, friends, and so on—have different expectations of him. Therefore, conduct in the performance of multiple legislative roles is likely to be highly variable, despite similar personality characteristics on the part of some legislators.

But how are personality characteristics in behavior related to recruitment into the legislative office? One might think that legislators who seek elective office and are willing to expose themselves to the common experience of repeatedly having to fight electoral battles might also share certain personality characteristics. These characteristics might distinguish them as an aggregate from those who do not cherish the uncertainties of the electoral struggle but seek access to important decision-making posts by appointment. Even here personality analysis may turn out to be negative for this reason: in political recruitment processes where large numbers of people participate in the choice of elective office-holders, the norms and expectations of the community are probably more relevant and decisive than the predispositions of those who stand for election. It may be less the candidate's real personality than his image that provides a more satisfactory explanation of electoral success.

Congruence is also likely to vary with the degree to which roles and role performance are institutionalized, standardized, and routinized. The more a role is institutionalized and role performance is secured through institutionalized sanctions, the less likely will behavior require the mobilization of energies rooted in the personality. Personality variables have no elbow room in which to function. This does not mean that certain personality types are not more suited than others for filling highly standardized roles. But it is probably the role that limits behavior rather than the particular personality that is attracted to the role.

We should not oversimplify the problem of congruence. For instance, the definition of bureaucratic roles is highly standardized, and the performance of bureaucratic roles depends on stable, disciplined behavior and adherence to prescribed rules. The kind of conduct that is expected is insured by appropriate attitudes that are transmitted, learned, and reinforced through institutional training. Now it is quite likely that the bureaucratic organization attracts personalities with predispositions more or less well suited to the kind of behavior that is expected and, in fact, rather severely enforced. It is probable, therefore, that though bureaucratic role performance may not be dependent on personality, recruitment into the bureaucratic role will be facilitated by appropriate predispositions. This, in turn, can lead to rigidities in bureaucratic behavior that, paradoxically, may obstruct the effective performance of the bureaucratic role. In fact, congruence of role and other aspects of personality in the recruitment phase may have dysfunctional consequences for the operation of a bureaucratic organization.

Congruence of role and personality is likely to vary, too, with the range of available behavior alternatives. In the American two-party system, for example, the citizen can vote or abstain from voting. If he votes, he can vote a straight ticket, split his ticket or perhaps vote for a third party. In general, his behavior alternatives are quite restricted. We can explain performance of the citizen role more economically in social or cultural than in personal terms. That John Smith votes Republican because all of his friends are Republicans or because he sees his interests better served by the Republican party is probably sufficient explanation of his behavior. If personality analysis should discover that he votes Republican because of a deep-seated hatred of his father who was a Democrat, and that his Republican vote has this (conscious or unconscious) meaning for him, we have an interesting bit of information that may be useful in understanding John Smith as a personality. It does not add very much to our knowledge of his political behavior. On the other hand, if we should find that John Smith votes Republican though all of his friends are Democrats, or that he votes as he does though his interests would be better served, even in his own opinion, by the Democrats, analysis of his political behavior on the personality level may supply a missing link in explanation. In short, analysis of political behavior in terms of personality seems advantageous if we are confronted with deviant conduct, deviant in a statistical, not a pathological sense.

There are other situations in which the relationship between role and personality may be accentuated and where relatively high congruence has significant consequences for the functioning of a political system.

High congruence may occur in connection with largely voluntaristic roles, that is, roles that are not solidly institutionalized. In Western democracies, for instance, the roles of rebel, hermit, or prophet are less likely to be

taken in response to others' expectations (though this element is ever-present by definition of role), but in response to strong motivations at the level of personality.
These roles are not only voluntaristic from an institutional point of view but also highly specialized. They call
for skills that are rarely transmitted in a cultural sense
and they allow a considerable degree of freedom in performance. In an institutional setting like a legislature, this
category might include the role of maverick. Individuals
with appropriate personality predispositions will take
and shape these roles. In their case, then, analysis of the
personal basis of political behavior in personality terms
may be very rewarding.

Personality may also be the decisive factor in role taking
and performance where a person is exposed to conflicting
expectations. How role conflict of one sort or another
is resolved can be analyzed in social or cultural terms
alone, of course. But it may also be a function of personality predispositions. For instance, withdrawal from political participation can be due to the neutralizing effect
of cross-pressures, an explanation on the social level of
analysis. But it can also be due to anxieties occasioned by
the conflict that are associated with similar experiences in
the formative stages of personality development.

Role and personality may approximate a high degree of
congruence in perceptually ambiguous situations in which
the actions, expectations, and sanctions of others in a
role relationship are blurred, for whatever reason. If no
stable points of behavioral reference are available and no
directional cues are forthcoming, the actor, unable to
cope with ambiguity in any other way, will define his
role for himself by falling back on personal values and
experiences that may or may not be objectively relevant
in orienting himself to others. While this behavior functions to resolve personal strains brought about by the
ambiguous situation, it tends to make for a great deal of
projective thinking, stereotypic responses, and irration-
ality.

Finally, roles allowing for a high degree of discretion

in performance may be highly congruent with other personality characteristics. The king who cannot do wrong, the authoritarian or charismatic leader, and similar roles are almost by definition predicated on the expectation that there shall be no expectations. In the absence of institutional sanctions, personality has much leeway to shape the role in socially and culturally unpredictable ways. Of course, there are limits to what incumbents of such roles can do. Autocrats have been toppled from power and prophets have lost their glamour. But the limits set to behavior in these roles are sufficiently vague to allow the actor to shape his social environment in line with his personality needs and predispositions more than is usually the case.

These examples of relatively high congruence between role and personality might give the incorrect impression that analysis of political behavior is confined only to them. The examples are exceptions to support the general proposition that in complex political systems it is difficult to postulate theoretically or discover empirically personality attributes that are invariably and inevitably linked to particular roles. On the other hand, it does not follow that recruitment into or performance of certain roles cannot at times entail the possession of appropriate personality characteristics. I am merely arguing that behavior in the performance of culturally validated roles on the one hand, and behavior in response to personality predispositions on the other, is sufficiently plastic to prohibit any kind of dogmatic assertion about the relationship between them. Some roles may attract certain personality types and limit access to other types. Other roles may occasion behavior quite independent of any personality characteristics. Congruence is a variable property of the relationship and always a matter of empirical determination.

The relationship between role and other aspects of personality is not easy to determine empirically because the behavior involved is elusive. Take, for example, what is sometimes called policy-planning. As conduct in the performance of a specific role, policy-planning requires the appraisal of many alternatives and even greater numbers of consequences flowing from these alternatives under conditions of more or less uncertainty. In terms of personality, an actor in an uncertain situation must be able to tolerate ambiguity. Persons given to undue anxiety, whatever its source in their life histories, are probably unable to live up to the expectations and demands made on the policy planner as a role type. I would think it extremely difficult to separate out those behavioral elements of policy-planning that stem from the condition of objective uncertainty and those that stem from subjective-personal qualities.

It is equally difficult to make a distinction between the function of personality in role recruitment and role performance. In some cases, as that of the organizer as against administrator, the roles are clear enough to make discovery of suitable personality characteristics relatively easy. Whatever they are, the personality features necessary for organizing are probably quite different from those necessary for administering. Indeed, in these cases high congruence between personality and role is deliberately cultivated in the selection of personnel. It may be difficult to find a single person who possesses the personality attributes deemed desirable to fill both roles simultaneously.

One final example suggests how subtle the problem is. Leadership is sometimes equated with dominance as a personality trait. It is fairly safe to say that a dependent or withdrawing person is unsuited for the role. But leadership does not necessarily require dominance at the personal basis of behavior. Congruence between the role and other aspects of personality is likely to be incomplete as well as variable, because performance of leadership takes place in response to social situations and cultural norms that may be quite independent of personality needs. Indeed if complete congruence between the leader role and dominance as a personality trait were to occur, it would in all probability have disastrous consequences for political behavior and the political system, whatever its ideological complexion. The resultant tensions between the demands of personality and social or cultural requirements for behavior would make any sort of political system unmanageable. Just as Hitler's hysterical and paranoid personality came ultimately into conflict with the realistic requirements of the system that he had created in his own image and doomed it, so a totally involved democratic citizenry, involved in the sense of being compulsively committed to participation in all decision-making, would probably doom a democratic polity. It is, therefore, neither necessary nor correct to interpret all political roles as more or less power-oriented in a psychological sense, or to expect, depending on the degree of power actually associated with a role, that only persons with the appropriate increment of power-orientation in their personalities can fit into corresponding political roles.

BIBLIOGRAPHY

PERSONALITY ANALYSIS

Adorno, T. W., Frenkel-Brunswik, E., Levinson, Daniel J., and Sanford, R. Nevitt, *The Authoritarian Personality.* (New York: Harper, 1950.)

Erikson, Erik H., *Childhood and Society.* (New York: Norton, 1950.)

Fluegel, J. C., *Man, Morals and Society.* (London: Duckworth, 1945.)

George, Alexander L., and George, Juliette L., *Woodrow Wilson and Colonel House.* (New York: John Day, 1956.)

Lasswell, Harold D., *Psychopathology and Politics.* (New York: Viking Compass, 1960.)

Wallas, Graham, *Human Nature in Politics.* (New York: Knopf, 3rd. ed., 1921.)

POLITICAL OPINIONS AND ATTITUDES

Eysenck, H. J., *The Psychology of Politics*. (New York: Praeger, 1954.)

Hyman, Herbert, *Political Socialization: A Study in the Psychology of Political Behavior*. (New York: Free Press, 1959.)

Lane, Robert E., *Political Life: Why People Get Involved in Politics*. (New York: Free Press, 1959.)

Newcomb, Theodore M., *Personality and Social Change*. (New York: Dryden, 1943.)

Saenger, Gerhart, *The Social Psychology of Prejudice*. (New York: Harper, 1953.)

Smith, M. Brewster, Bruner, Jerome, and White, Robert W., *Opinions and Personality*. (New York: Wiley, 1956.)

POLITICAL VALUES IN PERSONALITY

Dollard, John, Doob, Leonard W., Miller, Neal E., Mowrer, O. H., and Sears, Robert R., *Frustration and Aggression*. (New Haven: Yale University Press, 1939.)

Fromm, Erich, *Escape from Freedom*. (New York: Rinehart, 1941.)

Lane, Robert E., *Political Ideology: Why the American Common Man Believes What He Does*. (New York: Free Press, 1962.)

Lewin, Kurt, *Resolving Social Conflicts*. (New York: Harper, 1948.)

Mead, Margaret, *Soviet Attitudes Toward Authority*. (New York: McGraw-Hill Book Company, 1951.)

Money-Kyrle, R. E., *Psychoanalysis and Politics: A Contribution to the Psychology of Politics and Morals*. (New York: Norton, 1951.)

Murphy, Gardner, *In the Minds of Men*. (New York: Basic Books, 1953.)

PERSONALITY AND POLITICAL ROLE

Cantril, Hadley, *Human Nature and Political Systems*. (New Brunswick, N.J.: Rutgers University Press, 1961.)

Gerth, Hans, and Mills, C. Wright, *Character and Social Structure*. (New York: Harcourt, Brace, 1953.)

Gouldner, Alvin W. (ed.), *Studies in Leadership*. (New York: Harper, 1950.)

Lasswell, Harold D., *Power and Personality*. (New York: Norton, 1948.)

Lipset, Seymour M., and Lowenthal, Leo (eds.), *Culture and Social Character*. (New York: Free Press, 1961.)

Riesman, David, *Faces in the Crowd*. (New Haven: Yale University Press, 1952.)

CHAPTER FIVE

✵ ✵

BEHAVIORAL

DILEMMAS

The behavioral persuasion in politics is difficult to live by. Behavioral practitioners make exacting scientific demands on themselves. They encounter great practical obstacles; the dilemmas of behavioral inquiry are perplexing and often frustrating and the increments to political knowledge that any single piece of research may make are very modest.

But certainly, as one reviews the developments of the last fifteen years, roughly the period since the end of World War II, the contributions that behavioral research has made to political knowledge are impressive. There have been substantial advances in almost all the traditional areas of political science. Of course, the contributions are uneven in both quantity and quality. There are reasons for this unevenness. Many of these reasons involve very technical, methodological matters that are difficult to explain in simple language, and trying to state them simply may be somewhat foolish. My purpose here is to highlight some of the difficulties and dilemmas that make behavioral research in politics a venturesome enterprise, just as the prospects of solution represent the continuing challenge of the behavioral persuasion.

The behavioral persuasion in politics aspires to the status of science. Seeking this goal, it shares all the problems that characterize the scientific way of life, in the human as well as the natural sciences. Scientists and philosophers of science have written about these problems at length and I shall not treat them here. Nor shall I deal with those perennial questions such as what we mean by science when we speak of a science of politics, whether such a science is possible and, if it is, just how it is similar to or different from the other sciences, behavioral or natural. I take it for granted that a science of politics is both possible and desirable, and I shall start from there.

Another disclaimer is in order. I shall not deal with the ever-present mistakes and errors that inevitably occur in any research effort: errors of omission at the inception of a project, errors of commission in the process of research, errors of exaggeration in the use of over-refined research tools (where validity is sacrificed to precision), or errors of underestimation in the treatment of data (where the imagination is handcuffed in the name of validity). And I shall not deal with the endless frustrations experienced in chasing after respondents in a sometimes hopeless attempt to maintain the probabilistic purity of a sample design; in spending strenuous and often seemingly wasted hours to increase the reliability of a content analysis; in trying to develop alternate codes for the classification of raw data that will not violate either one's theory or the data; or in simply programming a meaningful analysis. The possibility of error exists all along the way.

Perhaps the first lesson which the behavioral researcher in politics should learn is to be candid about the limitations of his work. This does not mean he should permit sloppy work, but the researcher himself should point out flaws in his work that may be due to mishaps in the field, discrepancies in the data, mistakes in analysis, and so on. For nobody knows as well as he where and what the flaws are. There are usually legitimate reasons for difficulties and mistakes that are of scholarly interest.

I shall not attempt, then, either a systematic or complete discussion of all the dilemmas that I sense in behavioral research on politics. In the spirit of the essay form I have chosen, I shall only mention a few of the things that come to mind as they are grounded in my own experience in research.

OBSERVATIONAL DILEMMAS

Behavior is a series of acts through which man moves in time and space. It is a datum of observation but a datum that does not constitute a self-evident fact. Instead it is a fact that is given meaning by the observer in the very process of observation. Otherwise observation itself would be meaningless. And if observation had no meaning, it would not occur. Observation is itself a form of behavior that involves giving certain types of meaning to the object of observation, depending on who the observer is. This is true of the mother who observes her baby, of the tourist who observes a new landscape, of the astronomer who observes the movement of the stars, and of the political scientist who observes the action of a legislature or the behavior of voters.

Observation is as much giving meaning to the behavior that is observed as being engaged in meaningful behavior. The observer necessarily observes himself in the act of observing others. The extent of his success determines, at least in part, his success in observing others. This double aspect of observation makes it a scientific challenge.

Error in observation means that the observed act or behavioral pattern has been given false meaning. We say that the observed behavior has been misinterpreted. Whether the misinterpretation is willful or not, the false meaning is due to the behavior of the observer. The sources of error in observation—giving false meaning to the object of observation—are manifold. Their discovery has been a matter of interest to the philosopher, the theologian, the psychoanalyst and the scientist. Whatever the approach to the discovery of error, there is agreement that the reduction of error involves changes in the behavior of the observer, not of the observed. If the history of humanity is a history of errors, as some believe, the history of science is a continuing effort to reduce errors in observation.

The problem of reducing error in the behavioral sciences is compounded by the complexity of human behavior. The smallest observable unit of behavior, the act, is inordinately complex, even if treated as a biological or neurological phenomenon alone. How much more complex is the series of acts that constitutes the behavior of the human organism as a whole! And this complexity is compounded when we come to deal with man's behavior in his social relations. The observer's task would almost seem hopeless if it were not for one significant aspect of human behavior: the fact that man himself gives meaning to his multiple actions. Of course, a man may err in the meanings he gives to his own behavior. There may be quite a discrepancy between what he is doing and what he thinks he is doing. But it seems quite clear that the human dilemma need not be the observer's dilemma. The observer has one advantage over the observed: he can check and, in fact, must check his own meanings against those that the observed gives his own behavior. In this respect, then, the behavioral approach in politics has a decided advantage over those that describe and analyze actions without considering what these actions mean to the actors.

But this creates another problem. If our observations of political behavior are to meet the test of inter-subjective agreement between observer and observed, the meanings given to behavior by the observer and those given by the observed must be captured in a single structure of meanings that is internally consistent. This does not mean that their *language* must be alike. On the contrary, the scientific observer must use a language that is sufficiently abstract to contain the language of the observed. But clearly, the meanings, though expressed in different languages, must be consistent.

The meanings people give to their political behavior are critical data for scientific observation precisely because, from the standpoint of the behavioral persuasion, there is no "behavior as such" in a purely physical or mechanistic sense. Observation is a communicative act in which both observer and observed are mutually implicated. Whether these communicative acts are expressed visually, sensorially, or verbally, observation is impossible without communication, and communication is impossible without attention to meanings. This creates many problems of method in observation, for the existence of the communicative network not only binds but also affects both observer and observed. The necessity of attention to meanings is quite evident in the uses that the interview, which is the main tool of behavioral analysis, can be put to. The observer's questions and the observed's responses must be mutually meaningful. The communicative nature of observation is most obvious here. But the ability to hide an observer behind a one-way mirror or a hidden microphone does not negate the communicative aspect of observation. Without unity of meanings between observer and observed, there would be no communication and hence no observation.

Neglect of this two-way flow of meanings can seriously damage the reliability of behavioral research. Though it is now generally recognized that research must attend to latent as well as manifest meanings of political behavior, little progress has been made as yet in publicly defining the observational standpoint and the meanings of the investigator. I am thinking of something more than an explicit statement of the observer's theoretical framework and its scientific meaning-content, or even a clear statement of his goal values or policy preferences. What I have in mind is those often preconscious or unconscious meanings that may affect his observational stance. For even though two observers may work with the same formal-theoretical frame of reference or with the same goal values, they may still make different observations. I am not demanding that every behavioral researcher should expose himself to intensive psychoanalysis. I am only suggesting that sustained self-observation on the observer's part as he relates himself to the observed will considerably reduce what I feel to be a very genuine dilemma of political behavior research.

Training in self-observation is only the beginning of the behavioral quest for reliable observation. Part of the observational dilemma in politics, at least at present, is the backward training in research methods and techniques generally. Compared with the training in other disciplines, this training does not utilize the technological opportunities now available. Admittedly, the behavioral approaches in the study of politics are not exclusive alternatives to the more traditional historical, legal, or institutional approaches in political science. In the last fifteen years, most of those who have come to the behavioral persuasion in politics have been largely self-taught. Trained in the traditional techniques of political science, they had to develop new skills. Though much of the traditional curriculum in political science may have been a waste of time for them, their background in classical political theory, historical knowledge, and institutional concerns sensitized the new group of behaviorists to the observational dilemma. I sometimes feel that some of the younger practitioners of the behavioral persuasion in politics, impatient with this background, yet not in full mastery of the new techniques, lack the sophistication that behavioral observation requires. As a result, technological and methodological know-how is confused with knowledge that, in the case of political behavior, must include sensitivity to the dilemmas of observation.

The roots of the behavioral persuasion in the traditional foundations of political science are as important in the researcher's self-orientation as the novel developments in theory and method taken over from the other behavioral sciences. We cannot write off traditional approaches without understanding them. This means that the political behaviorist's training will be prolonged. Not only is he expected to master what is viable in the tradition of political science (over which there will be disagreement), but he is also expected to be familiar with the advances made in the neighboring behavioral sciences, with statistics and other empirical research techniques. These are demanding requirements, and relatively few are willing or able to survive such strenuous training. For this reason alone, the practice of behavioral research in political science will remain a very distinct and separate enterprise, at least in the immediate future.

The observation of political behavior is expensive as well as elusive. Even a very small study is extraordinarily time-consuming. The more spectacular analyses of individual political behavior reported in the last few years, analyses of electoral decision-making, legislative conduct, or community politics, involved teams of researchers, several years of field and analytical work, and considerable expenditures. At the same time, the financial resources presently available for political behavior research are limited. The result is that many behavioral studies appear unimportant. But a study's size does not determine its significance.

Just the opposite may be true. An empirical science is built by the slow, modest, and piecemeal cumulation of theory, methods and data. The importance of a study, no matter how big or small, must be judged in the total context of relevant research. The dilemma of behavioral research in politics is not scarcity of studies but absence of a cumulative body of theory within which new studies can be accommodated and digested so that as research proceeds, one can speak of an expansion of knowledge.

An abundance of studies does not make for cumulative knowledge. Studies may be inventoried and codified, but even if they are reinterpreted in terms of some comprehensive, theoretical schema, codification is no substitute for cumulation. Reinterpretation may do violence to the original intent of a study, and the dilemma of cumulative knowledge is confounded. On the other hand, the prescription that all research on a given substantive problem should be undertaken within the same theoretical framework is a counsel of perfection that is quite unrealistic in the present stage of development in political behavior research. There are too many competing theoretical approaches that are plausible and possible, and it will take a good deal more empirical work before any one theoretical orientation can be expected to seize the field. A theory's success is not legislated. It is proved or disproved by research.

It is difficult to disprove a hypothesis in political research. To be acceptable, it would seem to require much more replication—the independent empirical testing of theoretically derived propositions—than is practiced at present. Without a great number of retests, it is impossible to assess the reliability of proof or disproof; there is much professional prejudice against repeat performances. So-called originality rather than replication receives the kudos of the men of learning. It is difficult to find financial support for replicative studies. Graduate students doing doctoral research are admonished to come up with fresh contributions to knowledge. This is only part of the dilemma. The difficulty of maintaining sufficient controls over external conditions is more important in the long run. If conditions vary, changes in hypothesized relationships cannot be observed and measured. Replication seems worthwhile only if the analysis proceeds from hypotheses about the constancy of relationships among variables under like conditions.

Again, I am not proposing perfection. I am merely hinting at perfection to pinpoint a dilemma. Conditions in political life are rarely alike, but this is no reason for despair. It is probably enough if conditions are sufficiently similar to make replication worthwhile. If undertaken properly, comparative analysis serves in many respects as a substitute for more rigorous replication than is possible in laboratory experiments.

I do not believe experimental replication is impossible in political behavior research and I disagree with those who say that a rigorous science of politics is beyond our reach because human beings cannot be manipulated to suit the experimental needs of the researcher. However, I do not want to minimize the difficulties of experimenting with political behavior or institutions. Some very useful experiments in the stimulation of voting or with small groups, for instance, have been made in both laboratory and field settings. The difficulties of experimenting with people in laboratory or real-life situations are not due to obstacles inherent in the human condition. Medical research would not have made the advances it has made if people had not agreed to submit to experimentation. I believe the time will come when people will realize the advantages of experimentation for the prediction of policy consequences and will cooperate with behavioral researchers in the study of politics, as they already do cooperate in what is called "human relations research" in industry.

Experimentation in political behavior research will do more than facilitate replication and cumulation. It will also make available new data that can only be guessed at now. It is fashionable, especially among traditionally oriented political scientists, to belittle the psychologists whose favorite research site seems to be the college campus where students are available in abundance for testing or experiment. Yet out of the studies with college students have come new methods of inquiry now used by behavioral practitioners in politics in discovering and analyzing data that, until recently, seemed forever unobtainable. The application of scale and factor analyses to legislative roll-calls or judicial decisions has yielded data that were previously inaccessible, and these techniques have revealed important behavioral patterns that are related to institutional outputs. Sociometric techniques, first invented in the study of small, artificial groups, now make it possible to identify in great detail informal influence structures and processes in large institutions and even whole communities.

In other words, the availability of behavioral data is itself facilitated by new methodological and technical advances. The study of elections and electoral behavior was limited for a long time to the use of aggregate voting records alone. It was the systematic interview survey and probability sampling that brought the study of elections, which are surely critical democratic institutions, to the point where genuine explanation of variances in behavior became possible. We now take the probability sample survey so for granted that we easily forget the lack of behavioral knowledge about elections only a few years ago.

At the same time, behavioral research must be modest in appraising its data. Much unnecessary argument follows the lack of candor about limitations in the new kinds of data that are being made available. In view of the difficulties with direct observational techniques when it comes to the study of large groups, behavioral research must rely, of necessity, on opinions, perceptions, and verbal reports of behavior. The behavioral persuasion in politics cannot claim more for these data than what they are. For instance, sometimes research seeks to discover the influence attributed to certain individuals in a group, organization, or community on people or decisions. These data cannot be taken as evidence that these individuals are actually influential in general or in particular situations. Statements about influence or power based on measures of attribution are always inferential and this should be admitted frankly. On the other hand, I cannot accept the argument that influence attribution is altogether meaningless, and that it should be tested independently in some objective, factual sense. It seems to me that if such independent testing of influence were possible, the discovery of influence attribution would be unnecessary in the first place. The point is, of course, that apart from case studies it is very difficult, if not impossible, to discover influence or power as real, generic phenomena.

Moreover, perceptions may have consequences for observable behavior all their own, whether factually true or not. If I perceive another person as influential, I may well behave towards him as if he were in fact influential. If I find out that he is not, or less so than I expected, I will have "misbehaved," again with identifiable consequences for the political relationship involved. I will have to change my perception. Undoubtedly, attributions of influence are based on just such experiences and, for that reason too, constitute "definitions of the situation" that have a very real existence of their own and, therefore, are proper objects of behavioral investigation. Even a situation that is misperceived may be real in its consequences.

Perceptions may or may not correspond to reality, but as the determination of reality is elusive, they may have to serve as substitutes. They simply should not be made as statements about reality. The methodological problem is not the degree of correspondence between perception and reality. The problem is rather to decide just what degree of inter-subjective agreement among informants or observers should be accepted as constituting sufficient evidence for making inferential statements about reality. This is very much like agreeing on what constitutes an acceptable level of confidence in probability statistics. No injection of metaphysics is needed to cope with the problem of the relationship between perceptions and reality.

There are many problems which interest behavioral researchers in politics for which data continue to be scarce or inaccessible. Tool research, that is research not immediately concerned with new knowledge but with fashioning new techniques for gaining knowledge, is one way to come to grips with this. Tool research has not been very high on the agenda of political science and, so far, political scientists have mainly borrowed techniques from the other behavioral sciences. But there are problems unique to political science that require technological ingenuity.

Because political behavior invariably occurs in institutional settings, the size of the institution necessarily determines the number of subjects for behavioral inquiry. The political behavior researcher cannot ignore a small institution just because it is peopled by few individuals, for it may be a very important sub-system of the political system. But because the subjects are few, as in a legislative body, the number of analytical categories is likely to exceed available data. Multivariate analysis necessary to do justice to theoretical propositions cannot be pursued very far. The researcher has the choice of either reducing the number of his analytical categories or inventing an alternative way to handle his data. For instance, in a study of the legislative as a behavioral system, I found it necessary to develop a two-stage type of analysis that linked to each other the most frequently observed pairs of related variables, in this case role orientations, in a configuration of pairs until all most frequent pair relationships were exhausted. The researcher faces the dilemma of having to make a simpler and more unrefined analysis than his theoretical ambitions might call for. But even such relatively gross analysis is preferable to purely impressionistic linking of variables and treatment of complex phenomena.

As a final example of this type of dilemmas, there is the gap between case analysis and systematic analysis. Although a great many cases have been accumulated in different areas of politics, from the administrative process and legislative decision-making to party and pressure-group politics, the grounds for selecting the cases are somewhat obscure. In general, the substantive interests of the researcher and his convenience, that is, accessibility of documents and persons, seem to be the guiding criteria. These are hardly scientific criteria.

Most of the cases now available deal with exciting, spectacular, and perhaps critical situations rather than with more modal situations. As a result, the degree to which the cases are typical or not and of what universe of cases they might be representative is not clear at all. Then there is the question about the reliability of case studies. Would a second researcher, working with the same materials and dealing with the same informants, make factual discoveries reasonably similar to those of the first researcher, so that the findings cannot be considered random? I am speaking of findings, not interpretation in case studies. Few cases are cast in a theoretical framework that controls what goes into a case and what is left out. This makes it extremely dangerous to draw inferences from a variety of even presumably similar cases. Significantly, although cases are said to be rich sources of hypotheses about politics that are to be subjected to more rigorous and systematic research in the future, few follow-up studies of a replicative character are ever made.

In principle, there is no generic difference between the case method, the comparative method, and the statistical method. The difference between these methods does not lie in the data or in how the data have been collected. The difference lies in the nature of the inferences that can be made from the evidence in the use of these methods. If we grant that the inferences made in all three methods are probability statements rather than eternal verities, the difference lies in the level of confidence for the truth value of the statements that can be legitimately accepted as appropriate. I would argue, therefore, that all three methods are quantitative. If so, the inferences made by way of statistical techniques can be accepted with greater confidence than inferences made by comparative modes of analysis, and the latter are more reliable than inferential statements based on consideration of a single case.

This does not mean, of course, that one method is necessarily better than the other in some absolute sense. The method one chooses depends on a great many considerations, each of which influences the strategy of research designs. There may be disagreement with regard to a particular piece of research as to which method is most appropriate. All things considered, the researcher will choose the method that will yield the most satisfactory results. How to make the right decision is on another agenda of methodological discourse.

MACRO-MICRO DILEMMAS

The great issues of politics, war and peace, freedom and justice, order and revolution, and so on, require as much minute investigation as more modest problems. Political science is necessarily concerned with these issues. It has been in the tradition of the discipline to cope with them in molar rather than molecular fashion. As a result, there has been a misunderstanding between those interested in the great issues and those who settle for solving simpler problems. I do not believe that the broad perspective characteristic of large-scale policy studies is at odds with the microscopic inquiries of the behavioral persuasion. Indeed, linking different levels of analysis, the levels of individual or small-group behavior and the global levels of institution, community, or nation, constitutes a major unsolved item on the methodological agenda of the behavioral persuasion, and a challenging one.

The solution of the macro-micro problem is far from clear. The problem is, first of all, a theoretical one. Concepts of sufficiently high and abstract generality are needed to accommodate the multitude of levels on which political discourse can be conducted within a single theoretical schema. The theory must also be satisfactorily operational to permit empirical research on the level of the individual political actor. Recently schemata centering in concepts like decision-making and conflict have made progress along these lines. But not surprisingly, empirical research has been conducted in connection with issues where access to behavioral data is relatively easy. For instance, propositions derived from conflict theory can be more conveniently tested in research on metropolitan than international problems. Perhaps the issues of metropolitan conflict are pettier than those of international conflict, but because a great deal of behavioral research has been concerned with small rather than large issues, it does not follow that the latter are *ipso facto* beyond the range of behavioral inquiry.

Concentration of empirical research attention on areas where behavioral data are accessible makes sense if one respects the methodological difficulties of behavioral analysis on macro-analytical levels. If this has given the impression that behavioral investigation is possible only in areas where data are easy to come by, the impression is understandable but false. Because the problem of linking macro and micro levels of analysis is not simply theoretical but methodological, it would be sheer folly, at this stage of development, to seek solutions in areas where data are difficult to gather. Therefore, the behavioral researcher is well advised on strategic grounds to seek solutions of the macro-micro problem in research sites where behavioral research is viable. This self-imposed limitation of research attention is proof of strength, not weakness, in the behavioral persuasion in politics.

The macro-micro problem can be visualized as a dilemma of diverse, though continuous, observational standpoints. From this perspective, the distinction between macro units and micro units of analysis becomes relative. Small units like the individual or the small group, and large units like the organization or the nation-state, can be treated not as polar but as continuous variables. If this is so, all units, small or large, should be subject to ordering on a single continuum. Research can cut into this continuum anywhere along the line. In fact, this is what traditional analysis has largely done in concentrating on institutions as units of analysis. From the observational standpoint of a political system conceived as a macro unit, institutions appear as relatively small units. On the other hand, from the standpoint of individual behavior, an institution, even one as small as a committee, looms as a fairly large unit. A nation-state is a macro unit if looked at from below, and a micro unit if looked on from above (the standpoint of a regional system or the global community of states). The task of theory and research is to link these diverse units in terms of the segmental relations discoverable between them, whether vertical or horizontal, as parts of continuous sets of inter-locking behavioral chains.

As I have already suggested, such research is predi-cated on the availability of sufficiently general and ab-stract concepts that permit theoretical and operational linkages between and among different levels of analysis. Role analysis or system analysis, alone or in combination, is well suited to this task. For example, if *position* is taken as the basic micro unit of any institutional system, and *act* as the basic micro unit of any behavioral system, act and position can be linked, and with them the macro unit called institution and the micro unit called individual, by virtue of the *role* that an actor (the micro unit) takes in the performance of acts that are relevant to the position he occupies in an institution (the macro unit). Put somewhat differently, the macro unit institution now ap-pears as a role system that can be analyzed on the micro level of the individual actor.

Theoretically speaking, any unit of political analysis, whether large or small, depending on one's observational standpoint, can be thought of as a behavioral system of action related to other behavioral systems of action. Only if theoretical discourse is raised to this high level of ab-straction can we speak meaningfully of a relationship between an individual and an institution, or between a group and a government, or between a nation-state and the world community. Hopefully, such reconceptualiza-tion of concretely diverse units makes behavioral analysis possible on all levels and permits valid inferences from one level to another, without danger of traditional fal-lacies. To mention just two of these: there is the fallacy of extrapolation, i.e., treating micro systems as analogues of macro systems and extending findings from the micro-to the macro-level of analysis; and there is the fallacy of personification, reducing macro phenomena to the micro level of analysis, as in some formulations of national char-acter.

The problem is not one of immanent conflict between

individual and group, or between group and state, as
it is sometimes made out to be in normative political doc-
trine. Rather, from whatever point on the macro-micro
continuum one proceeds, the task of research is to build,
by patiently linking one unit with another, the total chain
of interrelations that link individual to individual, individual to group, group to group, group to organization, organization to organization, and so on, until one gives the
entire network continuous order. The use of behavioral
data in political analysis depends quite clearly on some
theoretical construct of the total system in which the individual actor is the basic empirical unit. I am not speaking of conceptual linkage alone, but of operational
linkage. The availability of the great issues to behavioral
analysis is clearly contingent on the solution of the
macro-micro dilemma.

The problem of using both discrete and aggregate data
in behavioral analysis is closely related. What may be true
of aggregates need not be true of the individuals who
compose them. There is a simple reason for this. It is easy
to make an incorrect inference when moving from statements about the behavior of aggregates, such as a national
electorate, to the behavior of any one person within the
aggregate. In other words, it is impossible to predict how
any one person in an aggregate will behave, though it is
possible to make probability statements about his behavior
if we know enough about the behavioral parameters of
the aggregate to which he belongs.

The use of aggregated data conceals much of the variance in the behavior of individual political actors that
the use of discrete data reveals. This does not mean that
statements based on aggregated data cannot be trusted
and accepted. Aggregate data are often the only kind of
behavioral information available for the purpose of making statements about groups or large collectivities. But
we should not make this necessity into a virtue. If we
want to make behavioral statements about large systems,
we still have the problem that aggregate data are evidently not sufficient. On the other hand, even if individual

data are available and are combined to permit statements about units larger than the individual, such aggregation may still do violence to findings about individual behavior. It has the advantage of showing how great the variance is that aggregate or broad institutional language conceals. But just what we mean empirically when we speak of a group's loyalty, a party's cohesion, or an organization's morale remains unanswered. Do we speak about a group property that is independent of the behavior of any one individual belonging to a group, party, or organization? Or are we really only speaking about the aggregated characteristics of individuals? The extent to which certain problems of politics can be subjected to behavioral analysis depends on answers to these questions.

DYNAMIC DILEMMAS

By all odds, the most troublesome of methodological dilemmas in the study of political behavior is the analysis of change through time. Most behavioral research in politics is cross-sectional, dealing with individuals, samples, or institutionalized groups at one point in time. Treatment of political change has been left largely to the historians of institutions, with the result that historical and institutional study in political science are often considered identical. This is unfortunate because, from the perspective of a science of politics rather than a history of politics, the analysis of change through time has as its goal not historical reconstruction but the discovery of causal relationships. Emphasis on change as a series of conspicuous, successive events often leads to spurious causal interpretation.

Behavioral study relies on talk, and dead men do not talk. Of course, it is possible to analyze changes in past behavioral patterns, or at least their symbolic expressions, by applying content analysis where documentary evidence is available. But this type of work is enormously time-consuming, and unless one is interested in historical patterns for purposes other than their own sake, the scientific yield is not likely to be rewarding. As a result, behavioral analysis of politics has been largely a-historic (though not anti-historic). The defense, or better, the rationalization, has been that, in any case, the task of behavioral research is to establish functional rather than causal relations between variables. This is a rather disingenuous avoidance of the causal challenge.

There is nothing intrinsically a-historic in the behavioral persuasion in politics. In fact, as cross-sectional studies accumulate, for instance, in the voting field, it becomes increasingly possible to study change and infer causation from the presence or absence of correlations. Comparison and correlation of cross-sectional studies made at different points in time are subject, of course, to the same limitations that characterize trend analyses of aggregate data. They permit identification of net changes in the behavior of the cross-sections, but they do not allow analysis of internal changes in the behavior of individual persons. The behavioral changes characteristic of individuals may be compensatory in the cross-section as in the aggregate; that is, changes in one direction may be offset by changes in the other. But the marginal results may indicate no, or little, change. Moreover, if there is too brief a period for which cross-sectional data is available, the time series constructed from the cross-sections is likely to reflect a sequence of unique events and again makes for spurious inferences about causation. However, in the absence of genuinely longitudinal information, comparison and correlation of cross-sectional data are still more reliable than global historical-institutional analysis based on spectacular occurrences. The analysis of cross-sections through time and through comparison is, of course, possible only if the data collected in different periods are genuinely comparable.

Longitudinal treatment of behavioral data is much more reliable in causal analysis than the use of cross-section through time. This type of analysis may range from a minute-to-minute account of the behavior of a single individual to the use of aggregate data where the unit of analysis is a well delimited territory. These are the extremes. At the present time, however, longitudinal analysis of political behavior at the individual level has been applied most successfully through the panel method. In this method, a panel of the same respondents is interviewed at different points in time. This makes it possible to observe changes in behavior that might otherwise be ascribed to intervening events like an election or a crisis. We can then ask respondents about these events directly and identify the sequence of cause and effect. Repeated interviewing of the same respondents is expensive, and for this reason alone the panel method has not been used as widely as it might. It has been used most often in before- and after-election studies, that is, over a relatively short period of time. But there is no reason to suppose that, given sufficient resources, it could not be used in the study of political behavior over a number of years.

Apart from cost, the main difficulty with the panel method of longitudinal analysis involves sampling. In order to investigate a sample over an extended period of time, the characteristics of the population-to-be—that is, the population concerning which statements are to be made—must be specified. Loss of subjects, or drop-out, and changes in the attributes of the respondents in the course of the study, such as age or economic status, make this specification of the population-to-be extremely difficult. It is probably for this reason that panel studies have been short-range, involving from two to four interview waves. This avoids technical difficulties stemming from changes in both interviewers and respondents. Other difficulties that will adversely influence spontaneity in answers to the same questions are "sample bias," arising out of differences in the characteristics of those willing to be interviewed several times and those unwilling; and "re-interview bias," that is, undue self-consciousness on respondents' part about being interviewed repeatedly.

Even in the face of these problems, the panel method is

the most promising technique for studying political behavior through time. Its application belies the contention that the behavioral persuasion in politics is necessarily anti-historical. It certainly is the most dependable technique for studying the process of cause and effect, for it permits description of the direction, degree, and character of change.

This suggests a subtle interplay between techniques of developmental analysis, logistic requirements of research, and theoretical formulations. If cross-sectional analyses are framed in terms of models that are a-historical, such as structural-functional or input-output formulations, adoption of these theoretical models has, in turn, tended to limit behavioral studies to cross-sectional techniques. On the other hand, theoretical models of change through time are rarely satisfied by cross-sectional surveys taken at different points in time. But the expensiveness of longitudinal research and other tactical difficulties have militated against much theoretical concern with political change at the level of the individual person.

We should not confuse longitudinal analysis or comparison of cross-sections through time (trend analysis) with those historical reconstructions of past events which characterize the chronological treatment of large-scale political phenomena, or with the equally historical reconstructions of individual life histories as practiced by psychoanalysis. Whether historians or psychoanalysts do the reconstructing, they provide important clues in understanding of change, but as statements about causes and consequences they are necessarily inferential.

Developmental analysis is perhaps the most exciting approach to the study of political change through time. Using this approach, the researcher deals with political behavior in the present by studying cross-sections in terms of whatever theoretical behavior model he may choose, but he does so against the background of both historical reconstructions and trend analyses, as well as against the foreground of whatever images he may build for the future. These are developmental constructs that emphasize the "from where, to where" sequence of actual and hypothetical events. Moreover, developmental analysis seems well suited to bridge the empirical world of the political scientist and the normative world of the policy planner.

BIBLIOGRAPHY

OBSERVATION, MEANING, COMMUNICATION

Boulding, Kenneth, *The Image*. (Ann Arbor: University of Michigan Press, 1956.)

Cherry, Colin, *On Human Communication*. (New York: Wiley, 1957.)

Kecskemeti, Paul, *Meaning, Communication and Value*. (Chicago: University of Chicago Press, 1952.)

Mead, George H., *Mind, Self and Society*. (Chicago: University of Chicago Press, 1934.)

Osgood, Charles E., Suci, George J., and Tannenbaum, Percy H., *The Measurement of Meaning*. (Urbana: University of Illinois Press, 1961.)

METHOD, EVIDENCE, INFERENCE

Buchler, Justus, *The Concept of Method*. (New York: Columbia University Press, 1961.)

Chapin, F. Stuart, *Experimental Designs in Sociological Research*. (New York: Harper, 1955.)

Durkheim, Emile, *The Rules of Sociological Method*. (New York: Free Press, 1958.)

Francis, Roy G., *The Rhetoric of Science*. (Minneapolis: University of Minnesota Press, 1961.)

Greenwood, Ernest, *Experimental Sociology: A Study in Method*. (New York: King's Crown, 1945.)

Lerner, Daniel (ed.), *Evidence and Inference*. (New York: Free Press, 1958.)

DESIGN, TECHNIQUE, STATISTICS

Chernoff, Herman, and Moses, Lincoln E., *Elementary Decision Theory*. (New York: Wiley, 1959.)

Goldberg, Samuel, *Probability: An Introduction*. (Englewood Cliffs, N.J.: Prentice-Hall, 1960.)

Hyman, Herbert, *Survey Design and Analysis*. (New York: Free Press, 1955.)

Lazarsfeld, Paul F., and Rosenberg, Morris, *The Language of Social Research*. (New York: Free Press, 1955.)

de Sola Pool, Ithiel (ed.), *Trends in Content Analysis*. (Urbana: University of Illinois Press, 1959.)

Selltiz, Claire, Jahoda, Marie, Deutsch, Morton, and Cook, Stuart W., *Research Methods in Social Relations*. (New York: Holt, 1959.)

Wallis, W. Allen, and Roberts, Harry V., *Statistics: A New Approach*. (New York: Free Press, 1956.)

HISTORY, CHANGE, DEVELOPMENT

Allport, Gordon W., *Becoming*. (New Haven: Yale University Press, 1955.)

Benson, Lee, *Turner and Beard*. (New York: Free Press, 1960.)

Goldfarb, Nathan, *Longitudinal Statistical Analysis*. (New York: Free Press, 1960.)

Lasswell, Harold D., *The World Revolution of Our Time*. (Stanford: Stanford University Press, 1951.)

MacIver, Robert M., *Social Causation*. (Boston: Ginn, 1942.)

Teggart, Frederick J., *Theory and Processes of History*. (Berkeley: University of California Press, 1960.)

❂ ❂

THE GOAL IS MAN

The goal is man. This is the ultimate justification for pursuing the behavioral persuasion in politics, as it is of any other human enterprise. Like art for art's sake, science for the sake of science has never made sense to me. This, of course, is a statement of value, and as such it cannot be scientifically demonstrated to be either true or false. In this regard, then, my understanding of the behavioral persuasion in politics rests on a premise that may be accepted or rejected but that cannot be proved or disproved.

But to say that the scientific study of man in politics has man as its goal is not saying very much, for men disagree on the nature of man in politics. Which is the man in whose service the behavioral persuasion finds its reason for existence? Is he a democratic man? A just man? A power seeking man? Is he a man who must be controlled because he is brutish and nasty? Or is he a man who must be liberated from the shackles of oppression to live a dignified life? These are philosophical questions better left to the philosophers. Whatever answer one chooses, there is likely to be a corresponding predicament. The most we can say is that different men have different conceptions of man and, as a result, give different meanings to what they do and why they do it.

I do not believe that the philosophical predicament need be a scientific predicament. Whatever philosophical views different scientists may hold about man and the reality of man, they need not interfere with their work in the laboratory or in the field. For there the validity of theoretical propositions about human behavior, from whatever philosophical position derived, is a matter of inter-subjective agreement, not absolutist assertion, and the reliability of observations is a function of measures that are inter-subjectively agreed on as well. The very existence of any scientific enterprise is predicated on inter-subjectively consensual rather than subjectively philosophical notions about man, reality, or universe.

Is the man in whose service scientists do their work a mere phantom then? Clearly not. For if "man" does not exist, there are many men, acting men, valuing men, goal-seeking men, and among them the scientist himself. If this is so, and if science is justified by its services to men, is it possible for science to be value-free, unconcerned with the values men cherish and the goals they seek? Can a science that seeks to maximize whatever particular values particular men prefer be neutral in a world of men who disagree? The issue has been debated for decades, with little agreement.

This should not be a source of despair. It does not mean that a science of man is impossible because behavioral scientists cannot agree on the relationship between empirical methods and their normative implications. Indeed, I believe that the very multiplicity of human goals and values makes the scientific enterprise, including the behavioral persuasion in politics, the challenge that is is. For it is because of the seeming multiplicity of values which men hold that behavioral science cannot and must not avoid dealing with the preferences, values, and goals of men. It does not follow that science cannot investigate preferences, values, or policy objectives because it cannot tell us what goal is best or what action is just. I do not believe that these things are any more inscrutable than more mundane matters of political behavior.

While ethics is a legitimate pursuit in its own right, it does not have a copyright on propositions of value. Logicians have long occupied themselves with the problem of consistency in the order of values. Behavioral scientists, in politics and out, might be able to contribute something as well. This something, I daresay, is nothing less than inquiry into the problem of the universality of values, a universality that any ethical philosopher must *assume* if he wishes his propositions of how men should conduct themselves to be accepted. I do not believe for a moment that the ethical philosopher engages in his search for what is wise, right, or just for its own sake any more than the scientist does his work for the sake of science.

In seeking to discover empirically whether and what universal values are held by men anywhere, the behavioral scientist proceeds from the same assumption as the ethical philosopher. Whatever success may accompany his search, it seems to me that he is in a better position than the ethical philosopher to pass judgment, not, of course, in his role as scientist, but in his role as moralist. As long as there is talk about man's common humanity, just as there is talk about man's inhumanity to man, the behavioral scientist cannot escape the task of determining what is human and what is not. But unlike the ethical philosopher he can say, "I have been there."

The question of whether a value-free science of politics is possible must not be confused with the question of whether a value-free science is desirable. The former is a problem of fact that, in the end, can be answered only through empirical research into the nature of science as a form of human activity. The latter is a problem of value that will remain open as long as scientists themselves give different answers. I think it will remain an open question for generations to come.

If a value-free science of politics is possible, it can be

put to the service of good as well as evil, of freedom as well as slavery, of life as well as death. In this respect a science of politics only shares the supreme dilemma of all the sciences, natural and behavioral. It would be most presumptuous to assume that political science has at its disposal a knowledge of good and evil, of justice and injustice, of right and wrong. But I believe that the position that a value-free science of politics is undesirable makes just that presumption.

It does not follow that a value-free science of politics is undesirable because it may be difficult to achieve. Values may creep into investigations of politics at almost any stage of the research process, from the selection of the problem to the interpretation of the findings. I don't believe that any clarification of the researcher's value biases will make his study any more scientific. I find it rather strange that some behavioral scientists, in politics and elsewhere, feel that if they only lay bare possible value biases, their research will gain in scientific stature. In that case, so the argument goes, any scientific appraisal of the research can discount the value bias and determine the degree of objectivity that has been reached. This argument strikes me as rather curious, because if the scientist is cognizant of his biases, it would seem to be up to him rather than to his critics to control them. If, on the other hand, he persists in proceeding with his scientific work though he knows it is biased, I can only conclude that he must find his practice desirable. He says, in fact, that he cannot eliminate his biases and that, therefore, he might as well live with them.

This stance should not be mistaken for the approach to the problem of values and scientific research on politics called policy science. The policy science approach does not assume that a value-free scientific study of politics is impossible because men pursue values through politics. Indeed, it sharply distinguishes between propositions of fact that are believed to be subject to scientific-empirical inquiry, and propositions of value for which empirical science has as yet no answer. But it does not deny that scientific research on propositions of fact cannot serve policy objectives; indeed, it asserts that political science, as all science, should be put in the service of whatever goals men pursue in politics.

In seeking to place the scientific study of politics at the disposal of the search for policy objectives, policy science need not violate the canons of scientific method. In fact, it is genuinely sensitive to the tensions and the subtle balance that exist between fact and value. Rather than confuse the two realms, it keeps them apart. If it did not make the sharp differentiation, we would soon have a "democratic political science," a "communist political science," an "anarchist political science," a "Catholic political science," and so on. Curiously enough, this absurdity is not altogether a phantasy. It is the inevitable outcome of the position that if only values are clarified, scientific research can move on its merry way.

It is more than likely that as long as men seek to impose their own values on other men, scientists will have to face the question of whether to place their services at the disposal of the combatants. Their answer will undoubtedly depend on the values they cherish as individuals with a moral conscience, but it will also depend on the institutional structure in which they are involved. The decision to serve group, class, nation, church, or world community, as one sees these collectivities, is always a matter of personal ethics. But whatever the choice, the scientific way of life is always dangerous. Even if the scientist sees his work as being in the service of goals that he himself cherishes, there is nothing in his science that prevents its being used for ends of which he disapproves. In this sense, at least, science is value-free. I don't think the scientist can escape this dilemma of having his work misused without giving up his calling. Only if he places himself at the service of those whose values he disagrees with does he commit intellectual treason.

BIBLIOGRAPHY

Ayer, A. J., *Logical Positivism*. (New York: Free Press, 1959.)

Bronowski, J., *Science and Human Values*. (New York: Harper, 1956.)

Frankel, Charles, *The Case For Modern Man*. (New York: Harper, 1955.)

Leighton, Alexander H., *Human Relations in a Changing World*. (New York: Dutton, 1949.)

Lerner, Daniel (ed.), *The Human Meaning of the Social Sciences*. (New York: Meridian, 1959.)

Lerner, Daniel, and Lasswell, Harold D., *The Policy Sciences*. (Stanford: Stanford University Press, 1951.)

Lynd, Robert S., *Knowledge for What?* (Princeton: Princeton University Press, 1939.)

Myrdal, Gunnar, *Value in Social Theory*. (London: Routledge and Kegan Paul, 1958.)

Northrop, F. S. C., *The Logic of the Sciences and the Humanities*. (New York: Macmillan, 1947.)

Weber, Max, *The Methodology of the Social Sciences*. (New York: Free Press, 1949.)

Zetterberg, Hans L., *Social Theory and Social Practice*. (New York: Bedminster, 1962.)

INDEX